D0429199

GOD'S
COVENANT BLESSINGS
FOR YOU

Kathy—
Let God be your "partner"
and comfort when you
need it.   Love & hugs,
Florann

God's
Covenant Blessings
For You

Compiled by
A. L. Gill

Harrison House
Tulsa, Oklahoma

Unless otherwise indicated, all Scripture quotations are taken from the *King James Version* of the Bible.

God's Covenant Blessings for You
ISBN 1-57794-069-5
Copyright © 1998 by A. L. Gill
Gill Ministries
P. O. Box 99
Fawnskin, California 92333

Published by Harrison House, Inc.
P. O. Box 35035
Tulsa, Oklahoma 74153

Printed in the United States of America.

Contents

Your Everlasting Covenant

**Part 4 — God's Covenant Blessings for
Successful Christian Living**

God's Covenant Truth Concerning:

Part 9 — God's Covenant Blessings for When I Need:

Part 10 — God's Covenant Word Reveals What He Wants Me to Do Today

God Wants Me to Understand His Covenant by:

A covenant is a serious, binding agreement, and the most solemn of all covenants are those sealed in blood. From the beginning of time, God has made and kept blood covenants with His people. In Deuteronomy we read, **Know therefore that the Lord thy God, he is God, the faithful God, which keepeth covenant and mercy with them that love him and keep his commandments** (Deuteronomy 7:9). In Hebrews, we read that Moses **sprinkled both the book, and all the people, Saying, This is the blood of the testament which God hath enjoined unto you** (Hebrews 9:19,20).

God's covenant promises greatly exceed the value of any other promises. A promise points to the future. Covenant promises point to the future based on Jesus' completed redemptive work in the past. By His death and the shedding of His precious blood, Jesus made possible our complete restoration to all that we have lost through sin. A covenant promise has the intrinsic ability to bring faith because it is based on a completed work. It is an absolute truth assured by the covenant-keeping power of His blood.

God's Word is certain and true. Whatever blessing He has promised, He will do. He has sealed His covenant blessings with the precious blood of His own Son. By applying His own blood, God has exalted His words to a place of unequaled, overcoming value. The absolute trustworthiness of these promises goes far beyond the limitations of mere words. God's blessings are established by His holy, inspired, unfailing, unchangeable covenant.

God's Word is alive and powerful. It cannot fail. As you read, meditate on and declare His covenant promises, faith will leap into your spirit, and you will receive the reality of those blessings into your life.

If you have not yet entered into a covenant relationship with God, you can do it now by praying the following prayer:

Father, I acknowledge that I am a sinner. Thank You for sending Your Son Jesus to die on the cross to pay the penalty for my sin. I renounce my past life of sin. I accept Jesus as my personal Savior. Jesus, come into my life and make me a new person. Thank You for forgiving me and cleansing me from all of my sin. Thank You for saving me and bringing me into covenant relationship with You through Your precious blood.

In Jesus' Name,
Amen

GOD'S
COVENANT
BLESSINGS
FOR YOU

PART 1

GOD'S WORD REVEALS MY COVENANT RELATIONSHIP WITH HIM

GOD THE FATHER IS:

MY COVENANT SOURCE

The Lord is my shepherd; I shall not want.

He maketh me to lie down in green pastures: he leadeth me beside the still waters.

He restoreth my soul: he leadeth me in the paths of righteousness for his name's sake.

Psalm 23:1-3

But thou shalt remember the Lord thy God: for it is he that giveth thee power to get wealth, that he may establish his covenant which he sware unto thy fathers, as it is this day.

Deuteronomy 8:18

Thus saith the Lord, thy Redeemer, the Holy One of Israel; I am the Lord thy God which teacheth thee to profit, which leadeth thee by the way that thou shouldest go. *Isaiah 48:17*

Beloved, I wish above all things that thou mayest prosper and be in health, even as thy soul prospereth.   *3 John 1:2*

And God is able to make all grace abound toward you; that ye, always having all sufficiency in all things, may abound to every good work.
                              2 Corinthians 9:8

The young lions do lack, and suffer hunger: but they that seek the Lord shall not want any good thing.   *Psalm 34:10*

But my God shall supply all your need according to his riches in glory by Christ Jesus.
                              Philippians 4:19

Delight thyself also in the Lord; and he shall give thee the desires of thine heart.   *Psalm 37:4*

God the Father Is:

My Covenant Provider

And all these blessings shall come on thee, and overtake thee, if thou shalt hearken unto the voice of the Lord thy God.... The Lord shall make thee plenteous in goods, in the fruit of thy body, and in the fruit of thy cattle, and in the fruit of thy ground, in the land which the Lord sware unto thy fathers to give thee. The Lord shall open unto thee his good treasure, the heaven to give the rain unto thy land in his season, and to bless all the work of thine hand: and thou shalt lend unto many nations, and thou shalt not borrow. And the Lord shall make thee the head, and not the tail; and thou shalt be above only, and thou shalt not be beneath; if that thou hearken unto the commandments of the Lord thy God, which I command thee this day, to observe and to do them. *Deuteronomy 28:2,11-13*

Therefore take no thought, saying, What shall we eat? or, What shall we drink? or, Wherewithal shall we be clothed? (For after all these things do the Gentiles seek:) for your heavenly Father knoweth that ye have need of all these things. But seek ye first the kingdom of God, and his righteousness; and all these things shall be added unto you.   *Matthew 6:31-33*

A good man leaveth an inheritance to his children's children: and the wealth of the sinner is laid up for the just.   *Proverbs 13:22*

For God giveth to a man that is good in his sight wisdom, and knowledge, and joy: but to the sinner he giveth travail, to gather and to heap up, that he may give to him that is good before God.
                    Ecclesiastes 2:26

GOD THE FATHER Is:

MY COVENANT STRENGTH

The Lord is my strength and my shield; my heart trusted in him, and I am helped: therefore my heart greatly rejoiceth; and with my song will I praise him. *Psalm 28:7*

The Lord is my light and my salvation; whom shall I fear? the Lord is the strength of my life; of whom shall I be afraid? *Psalm 27:1*

He giveth power to the faint; and to them that have no might he increaseth strength.

Isaiah 40:29

The salvation of the righteous is of the Lord: he is their strength in the time of trouble.

Psalm 37:39

My flesh and my heart faileth: but God is the strength of my heart, and my portion for ever.

Psalm 73:26

He said unto me, My grace is sufficient for thee: for my strength is made perfect in weakness.

2 Corinthians 12:9

I will love thee, O Lord, my strength.

The Lord is my rock, and my fortress, and my deliverer; my God, my strength, in whom I will trust; my buckler, and the horn of my salvation, and my high tower.

It is God that girdeth me with strength, and maketh my way perfect.

Psalm 18:1,2,32

Seek the Lord, and his strength: seek his face evermore.

Psalm 105:4

Trust ye in the Lord for ever: for in the Lord Jehovah is everlasting strength.

Isaiah 26:4

The Lord God is my strength, and he will make my feet like hinds' feet, and he will make me to walk upon mine high places.   *Habakkuk 3:19*

GOD THE FATHER IS:

MY COVENANT PROTECTOR

Many are the afflictions of the righteous: but the Lord delivereth him out of them all.

Psalm 34:19

The Lord is faithful, who shall stablish you, and keep you from evil.   *2 Thessalonians 3:3*

The Lord is on my side; I will not fear: what can man do unto me?   *Psalm 118:6*

For I the Lord thy God will hold thy right hand, saying unto thee, Fear not; I will help thee.

Isaiah 41:13

He [the Lord] shall cover thee with his feathers, and under his wings shalt thou trust: his truth shall be thy shield and buckler.

For he shall give his angels charge over thee, to keep thee in all thy ways.

He [the one who has set his love upon the Lord] shall call upon me, and I will answer him: I will be with him in trouble; I will deliver him, and honour him. *Psalm 91:4,11,15*

The name of the Lord is a strong tower: the righteous runneth into it, and is safe.
Proverbs 18:10

Thou, O Lord, art a shield for me; my glory, and the lifter up of mine head. *Psalm 3:3*

What shall we then say to these things? If God be for us, who can be against us? *Romans 8:31*

He will not suffer thy foot to be moved: he that keepeth thee will not slumber.

The Lord shall preserve thy going out and thy coming in from this time forth, and even for evermore. *Psalm 121:3,8*

GOD THE FATHER IS:

MY COVENANT STABILITY

The Lord reigneth, he is clothed with majesty; the Lord is clothed with strength, wherewith he hath girded himself: the world also is stablished, that it cannot be moved.   *Psalm 93:1*

He only is my rock and my salvation; he is my defence; I shall not be greatly moved.

Psalm 62:2

Cast thy burden upon the Lord, and he shall sustain thee: he shall never suffer the righteous to be moved.   *Psalm 55:22*

I have set the Lord always before me: because he is at my right hand, I shall not be moved.

Psalm 16:8

The Lord is faithful, who shall stablish you, and keep you from evil.   *2 Thessalonians 3:3*

To the end he may stablish your hearts unblameable in holiness before God, even our Father, at the coming of our Lord Jesus Christ with all his saints.   *1 Thessalonians 3:13*

The God of all grace, who hath called us unto his eternal glory by Christ Jesus, after that ye have suffered a while, make you perfect, stablish, strengthen, settle you.   *1 Peter 5:10*

Now to him that is of power to stablish you according to my gospel, and the preaching of Jesus Christ, according to the revelation of the mystery, which was kept secret since the world began.

Romans 16:25

Now our Lord Jesus Christ himself, and God, even our Father, which hath loved us, and hath given us everlasting consolation and good hope through grace,

Comfort your hearts, and stablish you in every good word and work.   *2 Thessalonians 2:16,17*

God the Father Is:

My Covenant Sufficiency

And he said unto me, My grace is sufficient for thee: for my strength is made perfect in weakness. Most gladly therefore will I rather glory in my infirmities, that the power of Christ may rest upon me. *2 Corinthians 12:9*

And God is able to make all grace abound toward you; that ye, always having all sufficiency in all things, may abound to every good work:....
Being enriched in every thing to all bounti-fulness, which causeth through us thanksgiving to God. *2 Corinthians 9:8,11*

Such trust have we through Christ to God-ward:
Not that we are sufficient of our selves to think any thing as of ourselves; but our sufficiency is of God. *2 Corinthians 3:4,5*

Bless the Lord, O my soul, and forget not all his benefits:

Who forgiveth all thine iniquities; who healeth all thy diseases;

Who redeemeth thy life from destruction; who crowneth thee with lovingkindness and tender mercies. *Psalm 103:2-4*

Blessed be the God and Father of our Lord Jesus Christ, who hath blessed us with all spiritual blessings in heavenly places in Christ.

Ephesians 1:3

According as his divine power hath given unto us all things that pertain unto life and godliness, through the knowledge of him that hath called us to glory and virtue:

Whereby are given unto us exceeding great and precious promises: that by these ye might be partakers of the divine nature, having escaped the corruption that is in the world through lust.

2 Peter 1:3,4

GOD THE SON IS:

MY COVENANT CREATOR

In the beginning God created the heaven and the earth. *Genesis 1:1*

For by him [Jesus] were all things created, that are in heaven, and that are in earth, visible and invisible, whether they be thrones, or dominions, or principalities, or powers: all things were created by him, and for him:
And he is before all things, and by him all things consist. *Colossians 1:16,17*

[God] hath in these last days spoken unto us by his Son, whom he hath appointed heir of all things, by whom also he made the worlds;
And, Thou, Lord, in the beginning hast laid the foundation of the earth; and the heavens are the works of thine hands. *Hebrews 1:2,10*

All things were made by him; and without him was not any thing made that was made.... He was in the world, and the world was made by him, and the world knew him not. *John 1:3,10*

And the Lord God formed man of the dust of the ground, and breathed into his nostrils the breath of life; and man became a living soul.

Genesis 2:7

Remember now thy Creator in the days of thy youth, while the evil days come not, nor the years draw nigh, when thou shalt say, I have no pleasure in them. *Ecclesiastes 12:1*

Thou art worthy, O Lord, to receive glory and honour and power: for thou hast created all things, and for thy pleasure they are and were created.

Revelation 4:11

GOD THE SON IS:

MY COVENANT SAVIOR

And we have seen and do testify that the Father sent the Son to be the Saviour of the world.

1 John 4:14

For God so loved the world, that he gave his only begotten Son, that whosoever believeth in him should not perish, but have everlasting life.

John 3:16

And she [Mary] shall bring forth a son, and thou shalt call his name Jesus: for he shall save his people from their sins.   *Matthew 1:21*

For the Son of man is come to seek and to save that which was lost.   *Luke 19:10*

Neither is there salvation in any other: for there is none other name under heaven given among men, whereby we must be saved.   *Acts 4:12*

Not by works of righteousness which we have done, but according to his mercy he saved us, by the washing of regeneration, and renewing of the Holy Ghost;
Which he shed on us abundantly through Jesus Christ our Saviour.   *Titus 3:5,6*

For all have sinned, and come short of the glory of God;
Being justified freely by his grace through the redemption that is in Christ Jesus.

Romans 3:23,24

If thou shalt confess with thy mouth the Lord Jesus, and shalt believe in thine heart that God hath raised him from the dead, thou shalt be saved.
For whosoever shall call upon the name of the Lord shall be saved.   *Romans 10:9,13*

GOD THE SON IS:

MY COVENANT LORD

Wherefore God also hath highly exalted him, and given him a name which is above every name:

That at the name of Jesus every knee should bow, of things in heaven, and things in earth, and things under the earth;

And that every tongue should confess that Jesus Christ is Lord, to the glory of God the Father.

Philippians 2:9-11

Likewise reckon ye also yourselves to be dead indeed unto sin, but alive unto God through Jesus Christ our Lord.

Let not sin therefore reign in your mortal body, that ye should obey it in the lusts thereof.

Neither yield ye your members as instruments of unrighteousness unto sin: but yield yourselves unto God, as those that are alive from the dead, and your members as instruments of righteousness unto God.

Know ye not, that to whom ye yield yourselves servants to obey, his servants ye are to whom ye obey; whether of sin unto death, or of obedience unto righteousness?   *Romans 6:11-13,16*

I beseech you therefore, brethren, by the mercies of God, that ye present your bodies a living sacrifice, holy, acceptable unto God, which is your reasonable service.

And be not conformed to this world: but be ye transformed by the renewing of your mind, that ye may prove what is that good, and acceptable, and perfect, will of God.   *Romans 12:1,2*

GOD THE SON IS:

MY COVENANT SHEPHERD

I [Jesus] am the door: by me if any man enter in, he shall be saved, and shall go in and out, and find pasture.... I am the good shepherd: the good shepherd giveth his life for the sheep.... I am the good shepherd, and know my sheep, and am known of mine. *John 10:9,11,14*

How think ye? if a man have an hundred sheep, and one of them be gone astray, doth he not leave the ninety and nine, and goeth into the mountains, and seeketh that which is gone astray? And if so be that he find it, verily I say unto you, he rejoiceth more of that sheep, than of the ninety and nine which went not astray. *Matthew 18:12,13*

For ye were as sheep going astray; but are now returned unto the Shepherd and Bishop of your souls. *1 Peter 2:25*

He shall feed his flock like a shepherd: he shall gather the lambs with his arm, and carry them in his bosom, and shall gently lead those that are with young. *Isaiah 40:11*

My sheep hear my voice, and I know them, and they follow me: And I give unto them eternal life; and they shall never perish, neither shall any man pluck them out of my hand. My Father, which gave them me, is greater than all; and no man is able to pluck them out of my Father's hand.

John 10:27-29

When the chief Shepherd shall appear, ye shall receive a crown of glory that fadeth not away. *1 Peter 5:4*

GOD THE SON IS:

MY COVENANT HEALER

Who hath believed our report? and to whom is the arm of the Lord revealed?

Surely he hath borne our griefs, and carried our sorrows: yet we did esteem him stricken, smitten of God, and afflicted. But he was wounded for our transgressions, he was bruised for our iniquities: the chastisement of our peace was upon him; and with his stripes we are healed.

Isaiah 53:1,4,5

For we have not an high priest which cannot be touched with the feeling of our infirmities; but was in all points tempted like as we are, yet without sin.

Hebrews 4:15

He [Jesus] cast out the spirits with his word, and healed all that were sick: That it might be fulfilled which was spoken by Esaias the prophet, saying, Himself took our infirmities, and bare our sicknesses. *Matthew 8:16,17*

Who his own self bare our sins in his own body on the tree, that we, being dead to sins, should live unto righteousness: by whose stripes ye were healed. *1 Peter 2:24*

GOD THE SON Is:

MY COVENANT RIGHTEOUSNESS

This is his [the Messiah's] name whereby he shall be called, The Lord Our Righteousness.

Jeremiah 23:6

My righteousness shall be for ever, and my salvation from generation to generation.

Isaiah 51:8

He [God] hath made him [Jesus] to be sin for us, who knew no sin; that we might be made the righteousness of God in him.

2 Corinthians 5:21

Not by works of righteousness which we have done, but according to his mercy he saved us, by the washing of regeneration, and renewing of the Holy Ghost;

Which he shed on us abundantly through Jesus Christ our Saviour. *Titus 3:5,6*

I count all things but loss for the excellency of the knowledge of Christ Jesus my Lord: for whom I have suffered the loss of all things, and do count them but dung, that I may win Christ,

And be found in him, not having mine own righteousness, which is of the law, but that which is through the faith of Christ, the righteousness which is of God by faith. *Philippians 3:8,9*

If by one man's offence death reigned by one; much more they which receive abundance of grace and of the gift of righteousness shall reign in life by one, Jesus Christ. *Romans 5:17*

Of him [God] are ye in Christ Jesus, who of God is made unto us wisdom, and righteousness, and sanctification, and redemption.

1 Corinthians 1:30

With the heart man believeth unto righteousness; and with the mouth confession is made unto salvation. *Romans 10:10*

The work of righteousness shall be peace; and the effect of righteousness quietness and assurance for ever. *Isaiah 32:17*

GOD THE SON IS:

MY COVENANT COMPANION

I am a companion of all them that fear thee, and of them that keep thy precepts.   *Psalm 119:63*

Sing and rejoice, O daughter of Zion: for, lo, I come, and I will dwell in the midst of thee, saith the Lord.   *Zechariah 2:10*

A man that hath friends must shew himself friendly: and there is a friend that sticketh closer than a brother.   *Proverbs 18:24*

Behold, I stand at the door, and knock: if any man hear my voice, and open the door, I will come in to him, and will sup with him, and he with me.   *Revelation 3:20*

Where two or three are gathered together in my name, there am I in the midst of them.

Matthew 18:20

He hath said, I will never leave thee, nor forsake thee. *Hebrews 13:5*

When my father and my mother forsake me, then the Lord will take me up. *Psalm 27:10*

Henceforth I call you not servants; for the servant knoweth not what his lord doeth: but I have called you friends; for all things that I have heard of my Father I have made known unto you.

John 15:15

GOD THE HOLY SPIRIT IS:

MY COVENANT COMFORTER

I [Jesus] will pray the Father, and he shall give you another Comforter, that he may abide with you for ever; Even the Spirit of truth; whom the world cannot receive, because it seeth him not, neither knoweth him: but ye know him; for he dwelleth with you, and shall be in you.

John 14:16,17

When the Comforter is come, whom I will send unto you from the Father, even the Spirit of truth, which proceedeth from the Father, he shall testify of me. *John 15:26*

Nevertheless I tell you the truth; It is expedient for you that I go away: for if I go not away, the Comforter will not come unto you; but if I depart, I will send him unto you. *John 16:7*

Know ye not that ye are the temple of God, and that the Spirit of God dwelleth in you?

1 Corinthians 3:16

Likewise the Spirit also helpeth our infirmities: for we know not what we should pray for as we ought: but the Spirit itself maketh intercession for us with groanings which cannot be uttered.

And he that searcheth the hearts knoweth what is the mind of the Spirit, because he maketh intercession for the saints according to the will of God.

Romans 8:26,27

The Comforter, which is the Holy Ghost, whom the Father will send in my [Jesus'] name, he shall teach you all things, and bring all things to your remembrance, whatsoever I have said unto you.

John 14:26

GOD THE HOLY SPIRIT Is:

MY COVENANT GUIDE

Howbeit when he, the Spirit of truth, is come, he will guide you into all truth: for he shall not speak of himself; but whatsoever he shall hear, that shall he speak: and he will shew you things to come. *John 16:13*

The former treatise have I made, O Theophilus, of all that Jesus began both to do and teach, Until the day in which he was taken up, after that he through the Holy Ghost had given commandments unto the apostles whom he had chosen. *Acts 1:1,2*

This is he that came by water and blood, even Jesus Christ; not by water only, but by water and blood. And it is the Spirit that beareth witness, because the Spirit is truth. *1 John 5:6*

This I say then, Walk in the Spirit, and ye shall not fulfil the lust of the flesh.

For the flesh lusteth against the Spirit, and the Spirit against the flesh: and these are contrary the one to the other: so that ye cannot do the things that ye would.

But if ye be led of the Spirit, ye are not under the law. *Galatians 5:16-18*

[I] cease not to give thanks for you, making mention of you in my prayers;

That the God of our Lord Jesus Christ, the Father of glory, may give unto you the spirit of wisdom and revelation in the knowledge of him.
Ephesians 1:16,17

I will instruct thee and teach thee in the way which thou shalt go: I will guide thee with mine eye.
Psalm 32:8

And thine ears shall hear a word behind thee, saying, This is the way, walk ye in it, when ye turn to the right hand, and when ye turn to the left.
Isaiah 30:21

GOD THE HOLY SPIRIT IS:

MY COVENANT TEACHER

But the Comforter, which is the Holy Ghost, whom the Father will send in my name, he shall teach you all things, and bring all things to your remembrance, whatsoever I have said unto you.

John 14:26

As it is written, Eye hath not seen, nor ear heard, neither have entered into the heart of man, the things which God hath prepared for them that love him.

But God hath revealed them unto us by his Spirit: for the Spirit searcheth all things, yea, the deep things of God.

For what man knoweth the things of a man, save the spirit of man which is in him? even so the things of God knoweth no man, but the Spirit of God.

Now we have received, not the spirit of the world, but the spirit which is of God; that we might know the things that are freely given to us of God.

Which things also we speak, not in the words which man's wisdom teacheth, but which the Holy Ghost teacheth; comparing spiritual things with spiritual.   *1 Corinthians 2:9-13*

Ye have an unction from the Holy One, and ye know all things.

But the anointing which ye have received of him abideth in you, and ye need not that any man teach you: but as the same anointing teacheth you of all things, and is truth, and is no lie, and even as it hath taught you, ye shall abide in him.

1 John 2:20,27

And when they bring you unto the synagogues, and unto magistrates, and powers, take ye no thought how or what thing ye shall answer, or what ye shall say: For the Holy Ghost shall teach you in the same hour what ye ought to say.

Luke 12:11,12

GOD THE HOLY SPIRIT IS:

MY COVENANT GIFT

If ye then, being evil, know how to give good gifts unto your children, how much more shall your heavenly Father give the Holy Spirit to them that ask him?   *Luke 11:13*

Then Peter said unto them, Repent, and be baptized every one of you in the name of Jesus Christ for the remission of sins, and ye shall receive the gift of the Holy Ghost.   *Acts 2:38*

Being assembled together with them, [Jesus] commanded them that they should not depart from Jerusalem, but wait for the promise of the Father, which, saith he, ye have heard of me. For John truly baptized with water; but ye shall be baptized with the Holy Ghost not many days hence....

Ye shall receive power, after that the Holy Ghost is come upon you: and ye shall be witnesses unto me both in Jerusalem, and in all Judaea, and in Samaria, and unto the uttermost part of the earth. *Acts 1:4,5,8*

And they [the 120 believers in the upper room] were all filled with the Holy Ghost, and began to speak with other tongues, as the Spirit gave them utterance. *Acts 2:4*

When the apostles which were at Jerusalem heard that Samaria had received the word of God, they sent unto them Peter and John: Who, when they were come down, prayed for them, that they might receive the Holy Ghost:.... Then laid they their hands on them, and they received the Holy Ghost. *Acts 8:14,15,17*

While Peter yet spake these words, the Holy Ghost fell on all them which heard the word. And they of the circumcision which believed were astonished, as many as came with Peter, because that on the Gentiles also was poured out the gift

of the Holy Ghost. For they heard them speak
with tongues, and magnify God.   *Acts 10:44-46*

God the Holy Spirit Is:

My Covenant Power

How God anointed Jesus of Nazareth with the Holy Ghost and with power: who went about doing good, and healing all that were oppressed of the devil; for God was with him.   *Acts 10:38*

The Spirit of the Lord is upon me, because he hath anointed me to preach the gospel to the poor; he hath sent me to heal the brokenhearted, to preach deliverance to the captives, and recovering of sight to the blind, to set at liberty them that are bruised, To preach the acceptable year of the Lord.   *Luke 4:18,19*

If the Spirit of him that raised up Jesus from the dead dwell in you, he that raised up Christ from the dead shall also quicken your mortal bodies by his Spirit that dwelleth in you.

Romans 8:11

I bow my knees unto the Father of our Lord Jesus Christ,

That he would grant you, according to the riches of his glory, to be strengthened with might by his Spirit in the inner man.   *Ephesians 3:14,16*

Ye shall receive power, after that the Holy Ghost is come upon you: and ye shall be witnesses unto me both in Jerusalem, and in all Judaea, and in Samaria, and unto the uttermost part of the earth.   *Acts 1:8*

And my speech and my preaching was not with enticing words of man's wisdom, but in demonstration of the Spirit and of power.

1 Corinthians 2:4

And when they [the early believers] had prayed, the place was shaken where they were assembled together; and they were all filled with the Holy Ghost, and they spake the word of God with boldness.... And with great power gave the apostles witness of the resurrection of the Lord Jesus: and great grace was upon them all.   *Acts 4:31,33*

The Angels Are:

Messengers of God's Covenant

And there were in the same country shepherds abiding in the field, keeping watch over their flock by night. And, lo, the angel of the Lord came upon them, and the glory of the Lord shone round about them: and they were sore afraid. And the angel said unto them, Fear not: for, behold, I bring you good tidings of great joy, which shall be to all people. *Luke 2:8-10*

And there appeared unto him [Zacharias] an angel of the Lord standing on the right side of the altar of incense. And when Zacharias saw him, he was troubled, and fear fell upon him. But the angel said unto him, Fear not, Zacharias: for thy prayer is heard; and thy wife Elisabeth shall bear thee a son, and thou shalt call his name John.... And Zacharias said unto the angel,

Whereby shall I know this? for I am an old man and my wife well stricken in years. And the angel answering said unto him, I am Gabriel, that stand in the presence of God; and am sent to speak unto thee, and to shew thee these glad tidings.

Luke 1:11-13,18,19

He [the centurion] saw in a vision evidently about the ninth hour of the day an angel of God coming in to him, and saying unto him, Cornelius. And when he looked on him, he was afraid, and said, What is it, Lord? And he said unto him, Thy prayers and thine alms are come up for a memorial before God. And now send men to Joppa, and call for one Simon, whose surname is Peter. *Acts 10:3-5*

And he said unto me, These sayings are faithful and true: and the Lord God of the holy prophets sent his angel to shew unto his servants the things which must shortly be done. *Revelation 22:6*

THE ANGELS ARE:

PROTECTORS OF GOD'S COVENANT

There appeared an angel unto him [Jesus] from heaven, strengthening him.   *Luke 22:43*

To which of the angels said he at any time, Sit on my right hand, until I make thine enemies thy footstool?

Are they not all ministering spirits, sent forth to minister for them who shall be heirs of salvation?
                                    Hebrews 1:13,14

There shall no evil befall thee, neither shall any plague come nigh thy dwelling.

For he shall give his angels charge over thee, to keep thee in all thy ways.

They shall bear thee up in their hands, lest thou dash thy foot against a stone.   *Psalm 91:10-12*

Be not forgetful to entertain strangers: for thereby some have entertained angels unawares.

Hebrews 13:2

He [Abraham] said unto me [Abraham's servant], The Lord, before whom I walk, will send his angel with thee, and prosper thy way.

Genesis 24:40

Behold, I send an Angel before thee, to keep thee in the way, and to bring thee into the place which I have prepared. *Exodus 23:20*

He [Jacob] dreamed, and behold a ladder set up on the earth, and the top of it reached to heaven: and behold the angels of God ascending and descending on it.

And Jacob awaked out of his sleep, and he said, Surely the Lord is in this place; and I knew it not. And he was afraid, and said, How dreadful is this place! this is none other but the house of God, and this is the gate of heaven. *Genesis 28:12,16,17*

THE ANGELS ARE:

WARRIORS OF GOD'S COVENANT

And there was war in heaven: Michael and his angels fought against the dragon; and the dragon fought and his angels,

And prevailed not; neither was their place found any more in heaven.

And the great dragon was cast out, that old serpent, called the Devil, and Satan, which deceiveth the whole world: he was cast out into the earth, and his angels were cast out with him.

Revelation 12:7-9

The angel of the Lord encampeth round about them that fear him, and delivereth them.

Psalm 34:7

Bless the Lord, ye his angels, that excel in strength, that do his commandments, hearkening unto the voice of his word. *Psalm 103:20*

And David lifted up his eyes, and saw the angel of the Lord stand between the earth and the heaven, having a drawn sword in his hand stretched out over Jerusalem. Then David and the elders of Israel, who were clothed in sackcloth, fell upon their faces. *1 Chronicles 21:16*

Then Nebuchadnezzar spake, and said, Blessed be the God of Shadrach, Meshach, and Abednego, who hath sent his angel, and delivered his servants that trusted in him. *Daniel 3:28*

My God hath sent his angel, and hath shut the lions' mouths, that they have not hurt me.
Daniel 6:22

And the Lord sent an angel, which cut off all the mighty men of valour, and the leaders and captains in the camp of the king of Assyria.
2 Chronicles 32:21

Satan Is:

The Adversary of My Covenant

Be sober, be vigilant; because your adversary the devil, as a roaring lion, walketh about, seeking whom he may devour:

Whom resist stedfast in the faith.   *1 Peter 5:8,9*

I heard a loud voice saying in heaven, Now is come salvation, and strength, and the kingdom of our God, and the power of his Christ: for the accuser of our brethren is cast down, which accused them before our God day and night.

Revelation 12:10

Satan himself is transformed into an angel of light.

2 Corinthians 11:14

Submit yourselves therefore to God. Resist the devil, and he will flee from you.   *James 4:7*

The thief cometh not, but for to steal, and to kill, and to destroy: I am come that they might have life, and that they might have it more abundantly.

John 10:10

And ought not this woman, being a daughter of Abraham, whom Satan hath bound, lo, these eighteen years, be loosed from this bond on the sabbath day?

Luke 13:16

The sower soweth the word. And these are they by the way side, where the word is sown; but when they have heard, Satan cometh immediately, and taketh away the word that was sown in their hearts.

Mark 4:14,15

Fear none of those things which thou shalt suffer: behold, the devil shall cast some of you into prison, that ye may be tried; and ye shall have tribulation ten days; be thou faithful unto death, and I will give thee a crown of life.

Revelation 2:10

Satan Is:

Defeated by the Blood of My Covenant

Forasmuch then as the children are partakers of flesh and blood, he [Jesus] also himself likewise took part of the same; that through death he might destroy him that had the power of death, that is, the devil.   *Hebrews 2:14*

And having spoiled principalities and powers, he made a shew of them openly, triumphing over them in it.   *Colossians 2:15*

And the God of peace shall bruise Satan under your feet shortly.   *Romans 16:20*

Put on the whole armour of God, that ye may be able to stand against the wiles of the devil.

For we wrestle not against flesh and blood, but against principalities, against powers, against the rulers of the darkness of this world, against spiritual wickedness in high places.

Ephesians 6:11,12

Nay, in all these things we are more than conquerors through him that loved us.

For I am persuaded, that neither death, nor life, nor angels, nor principalities, nor powers, nor things present, nor things to come,

Nor height, nor depth, nor any other creature, shall be able to separate us from the love of God, which is in Christ Jesus our Lord.

Romans 8:37-39

Behold, I give unto you power to tread on serpents and scorpions, and over all the power of the enemy: and nothing shall by any means hurt you. *Luke 10:19*

They overcame him [the devil] by the blood of the Lamb, and by the word of their testimony; and they loved not their lives unto the death.

Revelation 12:11

PART 2

GOD'S
COVENANT BLESSINGS
FOR SUCCESSFUL
FAMILY RELATIONSHIPS

THE COVENANT OF:

MARRIAGE

The Lord God said, It is not good that the man should be alone; I will make him an help meet for him. *Genesis 2:18*

Be ye not unequally yoked together with unbelievers: for what fellowship hath righteousness with unrighteousness? and what communion hath light with darkness? *2 Corinthians 6:14*

Nevertheless, to avoid fornication, let every man have his own wife, and let every woman have her own husband.

Let the husband render unto the wife due benevolence: and likewise also the wife unto the husband.

The wife hath not power of her own body, but the husband: and likewise also the husband hath not power of his own body, but the wife.

1 Corinthians 7:2-4

Adam said, This is now bone of my bones, and flesh of my flesh: she shall be called Woman, because she was taken out of Man. Therefore shall a man leave his father and his mother, and shall cleave unto his wife: and they shall be one flesh. *Genesis 2:23,24*

Marriage is honourable in all, and the bed undefiled: but whoremongers and adulterers God will judge. *Hebrews 13:4*

Whoso findeth a wife findeth a good thing, and obtaineth favour of the Lord. *Proverbs 18:22*

And he [Jesus] answered and said unto them [the Pharisees], Have ye not read, that he which made them at the beginning made them male and female, And said, For this cause shall a man leave father and mother, and shall cleave to his wife: and they twain shall be one flesh? Wherefore they are no more twain, but one flesh. What therefore God hath joined together, let not man put asunder. *Matthew 19:4-6*

Marriage Covenant Obligations of:

Husbands to Wives

The husband is the head of the wife, even as Christ is the head of the church: and he is the saviour of the body.   *Ephesians 5:23*

Husbands, love your wives, even as Christ also loved the church, and gave himself for it.

So ought men to love their wives as their own bodies. He that loveth his wife loveth himself.

For no man ever yet hated his own flesh; but nourisheth and cherisheth it, even as the Lord the church:

For we are members of his body, of his flesh, and of his bones.

For this cause shall a man leave his father and mother, and shall be joined unto his wife, and they two shall be one flesh.   *Ephesians 5:25,28-31*

Submitting yourselves one to another in the fear of God. *Ephesians 5:21*

Likewise, ye husbands, dwell with them according to knowledge, giving honour unto the wife, as unto the weaker vessel, and as being heirs together of the grace of life; that your prayers be not hindered. *1 Peter 3:7*

But if any provide not for his own, and specially for those of his own house, he hath denied the faith, and is worse than an infidel.
1 Timothy 5:8

Let thy fountain be blessed: and rejoice with the wife of thy youth. Let her be as the loving hind and pleasant roe; let her breasts satisfy thee at all times; and be thou ravished always with her love. *Proverbs 5:18,19*

Nevertheless let every one of you in particular so love his wife even as himself; and the wife see that she reverence her husband. *Ephesians 5:33*

Marriage Covenant Obligations of:

Wives to Husbands

Who can find a virtuous woman? for her price is far above rubies. The heart of her husband doth safely trust in her, so that he shall have no need of spoil. She will do him good and not evil all the days of her life. *Proverbs 31:10-12*

For after this manner in the old time the holy women also, who trusted in God, adorned themselves, being in subjection unto their own husbands. *1 Peter 3:5*

That they may teach the young women to be sober, to love their husbands, to love their children,

To be discreet, chaste, keepers at home, good, obedient to their own husbands, that the word of God be not blasphemed. *Titus 2:4,5*

I will therefore that the younger women marry, bear children, guide the house, give none occasion to the adversary to speak reproachfully.

1 Timothy 5:14

Nevertheless let every one of you in particular so love his wife even as himself; and the wife see that she reverence her husband. *Ephesians 5:33*

Submitting yourselves one to another in the fear of God.

Wives, submit yourselves unto your own husbands, as unto the Lord.

For the husband is the head of the wife, even as Christ is the head of the church: and he is the saviour of the body.

Therefore as the church is subject unto Christ, so let the wives be to their own husbands in every thing. *Ephesians 5:21-24*

A virtuous woman is a crown to her husband.

Proverbs 12:4

COVENANT TRUTHS FOR:

SINGLES

I will betroth thee unto me for ever; yea, I will betroth thee unto me in righteousness, and in judgment, and in lovingkindness, and in mercies. I will even betroth thee unto me in faithfulness: and thou shalt know the Lord.   *Hosea 2:19,20*

For thy Maker is thine husband; the Lord of hosts is his name; and thy Redeemer the Holy One of Israel; The God of the whole earth shall he be called.   *Isaiah 54:5*

I say therefore to the unmarried and widows, It is good for them if they abide even as I.

But if they cannot contain, let them marry: for it is better to marry than to burn.

But as God hath distributed to every man, as the Lord hath called every one, so let him walk. And so ordain I in all churches. *1 Corinthians 7:8,9,17*

He that is unmarried careth for the things that belong to the Lord, how he may please the Lord:

But he that is married careth for the things that are of the world, how he may please his wife.

There is difference also between a wife and a virgin. The unmarried woman careth for the things of the Lord, that she may be holy both in body and in spirit: but she that is married careth for the things of the world, how she may please her husband.

And this I speak for your own profit; not that I may cast a snare upon you, but for that which is comely, and that ye may attend upon the Lord without distraction. *1 Corinthians 7:32-35*

Delight thyself also in the Lord; and he shall give thee the desires of thine heart.

Commit thy way unto the Lord; trust also in him; and he shall bring it to pass. *Psalm 37:4,5*

COVENANT TRUTHS FOR:

THE ELDERLY

Rebuke not an elder, but intreat him as a father; and the younger men as brethren;

The elder women as mothers; the younger as sisters, with all purity. *1 Timothy 5:1,2*

Thou knowest the commandments, Do not commit adultery, Do not kill, Do not steal, Do not bear false witness, Defraud not, Honour thy father and mother. *Mark 10:19*

Honour thy father and mother; which is the first commandment with promise;

That it may be well with thee, and thou mayest live long on the earth. *Ephesians 6:2,3*

The aged women likewise, that they be in behaviour as becometh holiness, not false accusers, not given to much wine, teachers of good things;

That they may teach the young women to be sober, to love their husbands, to love their children,

To be discreet, chaste, keepers at home, good, obedient to their own husbands, that the word of God be not blasphemed. *Titus 2:3-5*

Those that be planted in the house of the Lord shall flourish in the courts of our God.

They shall still bring forth fruit in old age; they shall be fat and flourishing. *Psalm 92:13,14*

Likewise, ye younger, submit yourselves unto the elder. Yea, all of you be subject one to another, and be clothed with humility: for God resisteth the proud, and giveth grace to the humble.

1 Peter 5:5

And even to your old age I am he; and even to hoar hairs will I carry you: I have made, and I will bear; even I will carry, and will deliver you.

Isaiah 46:4

COVENANT TRUTH ON:

DIVORCE

They [the Pharisees] say unto him [Jesus],
Why did Moses then command to give a writing
of divorcement, and to put her away?

He saith unto them, Moses because of the
hardness of your hearts suffered you to put away
your wives: but from the beginning it was not so.

Matthew 19:7,8

I say unto you, That whosoever shall put away
his wife, saving for the cause of fornication, causeth
her to commit adultery: and whosoever shall marry
her that is divorced committeth adultery.

Matthew 5:32

The woman which hath an husband is bound
by the law to her husband so long as he liveth; but
if the husband be dead, she is loosed from the law
of her husband.

So then if, while her husband liveth, she be married to another man, she shall be called an adulteress: but if her husband be dead, she is free from that law; so that she is no adulteress, though she be married to another man.   *Romans 7:2,3*

Unto the married I command, yet not I, but the Lord, Let not the wife depart from her husband:

But and if she depart, let her remain unmarried, or be reconciled to her husband: and let not the husband put away his wife.

But to the rest speak I, not the Lord: If any brother hath a wife that believeth not, and she be pleased to dwell with him, let him not put her away.

And the woman which hath an husband that believeth not, and if he be pleased to dwell with her, let her not leave him.

For the unbelieving husband is sanctified by the wife, and the unbelieving wife is sanctified by the husband: else were your children unclean; but now are they holy.

But if the unbelieving depart, let him depart.

1 Corinthians 7:10-15

COVENANT BLESSINGS FOR:

AN UNSAVED SPOUSE

Believe on the Lord Jesus Christ, and thou shalt be saved, and thy house. *Acts 16:31*

Likewise, ye wives, be in subjection to your own husbands; that, if any obey not the word, they also may without the word be won by the conversation of the wives;
Likewise, ye husbands, dwell with them according to knowledge, giving honour unto the wife, as unto the weaker vessel, and as being heirs together of the grace of life; that your prayers be not hindered. *1 Peter 3:1,7*

To the rest speak I, not the Lord: If any brother hath a wife that believeth not, and she be pleased to dwell with him, let him not put her away.

And the woman which hath an husband that believeth not, and if he be pleased to dwell with her, let her not leave him.

For the unbelieving husband is sanctified by the wife, and the unbelieving wife is sanctified by the husband: else were your children unclean; but now are they holy.

But if the unbelieving depart, let him depart. A brother or a sister is not under bondage in such cases: but God hath called us to peace.

For what knowest thou, O wife, whether thou shalt save thy husband? or how knowest thou, O man, whether thou shalt save thy wife?

1 Corinthians 7:12-16

Thus saith the Lord, Keep ye judgment, and do justice: for my salvation is near to come.

Isaiah 56:1

Cast thy burden upon the Lord, and he shall sustain thee: he shall never suffer the righteous to be moved.   *Psalm 55:22*

COVENANT BLESSINGS FOR:

CHILDREN

Jesus said, Suffer little children, and forbid them not, to come unto me: for of such is the kingdom of heaven.   *Matthew 19:14*

He took a child, and set him in the midst of them: and when he had taken him in his arms, he said unto them, Whosoever shall receive one of such children in my name, receiveth me: and whosoever shall receive me, receiveth not me, but him that sent me.   *Mark 9:36,37*

Children's children are the crown of old men; and the glory of children are their fathers.

Proverbs 17:6

Ye fathers, provoke not your children to wrath: but bring them up in the nurture and admonition of the Lord.   *Ephesians 6:4*

Thy wife shall be as a fruitful vine by the sides of thine house: thy children like olive plants round about thy table.

Behold, that thus shall the man be blessed that feareth the Lord. *Psalm 128:3,4*

And these words, which I command thee this day, shall be in thine heart: And thou shalt teach them diligently unto thy children, and shalt talk of them when thou sittest in thine house, and when thou walkest by the way, and when thou liest down, and when thou risest up.

Deuteronomy 6:6,7

Lo, children are an heritage of the Lord: and the fruit of the womb is his reward.

As arrows are in the hand of a mighty man; so are children of the youth. Happy is the man that hath his quiver full of them. *Psalm 127:3-5*

COVENANT BLESSINGS FOR:

CHILDLESS COUPLES

He maketh the barren woman to keep house, and to be a joyful mother of children. Praise ye the Lord.   *Psalm 113:9*

Sing, O barren, thou that didst not bear; break forth into singing, and cry aloud, thou that didst not travail with child: for more are the children of the desolate than the children of the married wife, saith the Lord.   *Isaiah 54:1*

Blessed is every one that feareth the Lord; that walketh in his ways.

For thou shalt eat the labour of thine hands: happy shalt thou be, and it shall be well with thee.

Thy wife shall be as a fruitful vine by the sides of thine house: thy children like olive plants round about thy table.   *Psalm 128:1-3*

Lo, children are an heritage of the Lord: and the fruit of the womb is his reward. *Psalm 127:3*

Through faith also Sara herself received strength to conceive seed, and was delivered of a child when she was past age, because she judged him faithful who had promised. *Hebrews 11:11*

Christ hath redeemed us from the curse of the law, being made a curse for us: for it is written, Cursed is every one that hangeth on a tree:
That the blessing of Abraham might come on the Gentiles through Jesus Christ; that we might receive the promise of the Spirit through faith.
Galatians 3:13,14

His seed shall be mighty upon earth: the generation of the upright shall be blessed.
Psalm 112:2

COVENANT BLESSINGS FOR:

UNSAVED CHILDREN

Train up a child in the way he should go: and when he is old, he will not depart from it.

Proverbs 22:6

Even so it is not the will of your Father which is in heaven, that one of these little ones should perish. *Matthew 18:14*

...Send men to Joppa, and call for Simon, whose surname is Peter; Who shall tell thee words, whereby thou and all thy house shall be saved.

Acts 11:13,14

Believe on the Lord Jesus Christ, and thou shalt be saved, and thy house. *Acts 16:31*

The Lord is not slack concerning his promise, as some men count slackness; but is longsuffering to us-ward, not willing that any should perish, but that all should come to repentance.

2 Peter 3:9

Observe and hear all these words which I command thee, that it may go well with thee, and with thy children after thee for ever, when thou doest that which is good and right in the sight of the Lord thy God. *Deuteronomy 12:28*

I will pour my spirit upon thy seed, and my blessing upon thine offspring. *Isaiah 44:3*

But the mercy of the Lord is from everlasting to everlasting upon them that fear him, and his righteousness unto children's children.

Psalm 103:17

Thus saith the Lord, Keep ye judgment, and do justice: for my salvation is near to come, and my righteousness to be revealed. *Isaiah 56:1*

And all thy children shall be taught of the Lord; and great shall be the peace of thy children.

Isaiah 54:13

COVENANT BLESSINGS FOR:

WORKING WOMEN

Who can find a virtuous woman? for her price is far above rubies.... She seeketh wool, and flax, and worketh willingly with her hands.... She considereth a field, and buyeth it: with the fruit of her hands she planteth a vineyard.... She perceiveth that her merchandise is good: her candle goeth not out by night.... She maketh fine linen, and selleth it; and delivereth girdles unto the merchant.... Favour is deceitful, and beauty is vain: but a woman that feareth the Lord, she shall be praised.   *Proverbs 31:10,13,16,18,24,30*

And all the women that were wise hearted did spin with their hands, and brought that which they had spun, both of blue, and of purple, and of scarlet, and of fine linen.   *Exodus 35:25*

And a certain woman named Lydia, a seller of purple, of the city of Thyatira, which worshipped God, heard us: whose heart the Lord opened, that she attended unto the things which were spoken of Paul.   *Acts 16:14*

And Deborah, a prophetess, the wife of Lapidoth, she judged Israel at that time.... And the children of Israel came up to her for judgment.
                                        Judges 4:4,5

Ruth the Moabitess said unto Naomi, Let me now go to the field, and glean ears of corn after him in whose sight I shall find grace....

And Boaz answered and said unto her, It hath fully been shewed me, all that thou hast done unto thy mother in law since the death of thine husband:.... The Lord recompense thy work, and a full reward be given thee of the Lord God of Israel, under whose wings thou art come to trust.
                                        Ruth 2:2,11,12

COVENANT BLESSINGS FOR:

THE WIDOWS AND FATHERLESS

Pure religion and undefiled before God and the Father is this, To visit the fatherless and widows in their affliction, and to keep himself unspotted from the world.   *James 1:27*

The Lord preserveth the strangers; he relieveth the fatherless and widow.   *Psalm 146:9*

Leave thy fatherless children, I will preserve them alive; and let thy widows trust in me.

Jeremiah 49:11

Honour widows that are widows indeed.
Now she that is a widow indeed, and desolate, trusteth in God, and continueth in supplications and prayers night and day.   *1 Timothy 5:3,5*

Thou art the helper of the fatherless.
Psalm 10:14

Ye shall not afflict any widow, or fatherless child. If thou afflict them in any wise, and they cry at all unto me, I will surely hear their cry.
Exodus 22:22,23

Fear not; for thou shalt not be ashamed: neither be thou confounded; for thou shalt not be put to shame: for thou shalt forget the shame of thy youth, and shalt not remember the reproach of thy widowhood any more. For thy Maker is thine husband.
Isaiah 54:4,5

...I delivered the poor that cried, and the fatherless, and him that had none to help him.

The blessing of him that was ready to perish came upon me: and I caused the widow's heart to sing for joy.
Job 29:12,13

A father of the fatherless, and a judge of the widows, is God in his holy habitation. *Psalm 68:5*

COVENANT OBLIGATIONS OF:

PARENTS TO CHILDREN

And these words, which I command thee this day, shall be in thine heart: And thou shalt teach them diligently unto thy children, and shalt talk of them when thou sittest in thine house, and when thou walkest by the way, and when thou liest down, and when thou risest up. And thou shalt bind them for a sign upon thine hand, and they shall be as frontlets between thine eyes. And thou shalt write them upon the posts of thy house, and on thy gates.   *Deuteronomy 6:6-9*

And, ye fathers, provoke not your children to wrath: but bring them up in the nurture and admonition of the Lord.   *Ephesians 6:4*

Train up a child in the way he should go: and when he is old, he will not depart from it.

Proverbs 22:6

One that ruleth well his own house, having his children in subjection with all gravity.

1 Timothy 3:4

And he shall turn the heart of the fathers to the children, and the heart of the children to their fathers.

Malachi 4:6

And Jesus called a little child unto him, and set him in the midst of them, And said, Verily I say unto you, Except ye be converted, and become as little children, ye shall not enter into the kingdom of heaven. Whosoever therefore shall humble himself as this little child, the same is greatest in the kingdom of heaven. And whoso shall receive one such little child in my name receiveth me. But whoso shall offend one of these little ones which believe in me, it were better for him that a millstone were hanged about his neck, and that he were drowned in the depth of the sea.

Matthew 18:2-6

Covenant Obligations of:

Children to Parents

Children, obey your parents in the Lord: for this is right.

Honour thy father and mother; which is the first commandment with promise;

That it may be well with thee, and thou mayest live long on the earth. *Ephesians 6:1-3*

Children, obey your parents in all things: for this is well pleasing unto the Lord.

Colossians 3:20

Honour thy father and thy mother: that thy days may be long upon the land which the Lord thy God giveth thee. *Exodus 20:12*

My son, hear the instruction of thy father, and forsake not the law of thy mother:

For they shall be an ornament of grace unto thy head, and chains about thy neck.   *Proverbs 1:8,9*

Thou knowest the commandments...Honour thy father and mother.   *Mark 10:19*

Hear, ye children, the instruction of a father, and attend to know understanding. *Proverbs 4:1*

My son, despise not the chastening of the Lord; neither be weary of his correction: For whom the Lord loveth he correcteth; even as a father the son in whom he delighteth.   *Proverbs 3:11,12*

Hearken unto thy father that begat thee, and despise not thy mother when she is old.

Thy father and thy mother shall be glad, and she that bare thee shall rejoice.   *Proverbs 23:22,25*

Honour thy father and thy mother, as the Lord thy God hath commanded thee; that thy days may be prolonged, and that it may go well with thee.

Deuteronomy 5:16

GOD'S COVENANT INSTRUCTION FOR:

TRAINING CHILDREN

I know him, that he will command his children and his household after him, and they shall keep the way of the Lord, to do justice and judgment; that the Lord may bring upon Abraham that which he hath spoken of him.   *Genesis 18:19*

Train up a child in the way he should go: and when he is old, he will not depart from it.

Proverbs 22:6

He that spareth his rod hateth his son: but he that loveth him chasteneth him betimes.

Proverbs 13:24

Withhold not correction from the child: for if thou beatest him with the rod, he shall not die.

Proverbs 23:13

Foolishness is bound in the heart of a child; but the rod of correction shall drive it far from him.

Proverbs 22:15

The rod and reproof give wisdom: but a child left to himself bringeth his mother to shame.

Correct thy son, and he shall give thee rest; yea, he shall give delight unto thy soul.

Proverbs 29:15,17

Chasten thy son while there is hope, and let not thy soul spare for his crying. *Proverbs 19:18*

Whom the Lord loveth he correcteth; even as a father the son in whom he delighteth.

Proverbs 3:12

Fathers, provoke not your children to anger, lest they be discouraged. *Colossians 3:21*

Ye fathers, provoke not your children to wrath: but bring them up in the nurture and admonition of the Lord. *Ephesians 6:4*

All thy children shall be taught of the Lord; and great shall be the peace of thy children.

Isaiah 54:13

GOD'S COVENANT LAWS AGAINST:

ABORTION

Thou hast possessed my reins: thou hast covered me in my mother's womb.

I will praise thee; for I am fearfully and wonderfully made: marvellous are thy works; and that my soul knoweth right well.

My substance was not hid from thee, when I was made in secret, and curiously wrought in the lowest parts of the earth.   *Psalm 139:13-15*

...Bring my sons from far, and my daughters from the ends of the earth; Even every one that is called by my name: for I have created him for my glory, I have formed him; yea, I have made him.

This people have I formed for myself; they shall shew forth my praise.   *Isaiah 43:6,7,21*

And now, saith the Lord that formed me from the womb....   *Isaiah 49:5*

Then the word of the Lord came unto me, saying, Before I formed thee in the belly I knew thee; and before thou camest forth out of the womb I sanctified thee, and I ordained thee a prophet unto the nations.   *Jeremiah 1:4,5*

Lo, children are an heritage of the Lord: and the fruit of the womb is his reward. *Psalm 127:3*

He shall be great in the sight of the Lord, and shall drink neither wine nor strong drink; and he shall be filled with the Holy Ghost, even from his mother's womb.   *Luke 1:15*

Keep thee far from a false matter; and the innocent and righteous slay thou not: for I will not justify the wicked.   *Exodus 23:7*

If we confess our sins, he is faithful and just to forgive us our sins, and to cleanse us from all unrighteousness.   *1 John 1:9*

God's Covenant Laws Against:

Child Abuse

O Jerusalem, Jerusalem, thou that killest the prophets, and stonest them which are sent unto thee, how often would I have gathered thy children together, even as a hen gathereth her chickens under her wings, and ye would not!

Matthew 23:37

Ye fathers, provoke not your children to wrath: but bring them up in the nurture and admonition of the Lord.

Ephesians 6:4

They brought young children to him, that he should touch them: and his disciples rebuked those that brought them. But when Jesus saw it, he was much displeased, and said unto them, Suffer the little children to come unto me, and forbid them not: for of such is the kingdom of God.

Mark 10:13,14

Whoso shall receive one such little child in my name receiveth me. But whoso shall offend one of these little ones which believe in me, it were better for him that a millstone were hanged about his neck, and that he were drowned in the depth of the sea.

Woe unto the world because of offences! for it must needs be that offences come; but woe to that man by whom the offence cometh!

Matthew 18:5-7

Take heed that ye despise not one of these little ones; for I say unto you, That in heaven their angels do always behold the face of my Father which is in heaven. *Matthew 18:10*

Whosoever shall give to drink unto one of these little ones a cup of cold water only in the name of a disciple, verily I say unto you, he shall in no wise lose his reward. *Matthew 10:42*

COVENANT COMFORT FOR:

THE DEATH OF LOVED ONES

Precious in the sight of the Lord is the death of his saints. *Psalm 116:15*

For if we believe that Jesus died and rose again, even so them also which sleep in Jesus will God bring with him.

For this we say unto you by the word of the Lord, that we which are alive and remain unto the coming of the Lord shall not prevent them which are asleep.

For the Lord himself shall descend from heaven with a shout, with the voice of the archangel, and with the trump of God: and the dead in Christ shall rise first:

Then we which are alive and remain shall be caught up together with them in the clouds to meet the Lord in the air: and so shall we ever be with the Lord.

Wherefore comfort one another with these words. *1 Thessalonians 4:14-18*

I heard a voice from heaven saying unto me, Write, Blessed are the dead which die in the Lord from henceforth: Yea, saith the Spirit, that they may rest from their labours; and their works do follow them. *Revelation 14:13*

In a moment, in the twinkling of an eye, at the last trump: for the trumpet shall sound, and the dead shall be raised incorruptible, and we shall be changed.

For this corruptible must put on incorruption, and this mortal must put on immortality.

So when this corruptible shall have put on incorruption, and this mortal shall have put on immortality, then shall be brought to pass the saying that is written, Death is swallowed up in victory.

O death, where is thy sting? O grave, where is thy victory? *1 Corinthians 15:52-55*

GOD'S
COVENANT
BLESSINGS
FOR YOU

PART 3

GOD'S
COVENANT BLESSINGS
FOR SUCCESSFUL
RELATIONSHIPS

GOD'S COVENANT WORD
CONCERNING:

CHURCH

As we have many members in one body, and all members have not the same office:

So we, being many, are one body in Christ, and every one members one of another.

Romans 12:4,5

Not forsaking the assembling of ourselves together, as the manner of some is; but exhorting one another: and so much the more, as ye see the day approaching. *Hebrews 10:25*

Obey them that have the rule over you, and submit yourselves: for they watch for your souls, as they that must give account, that they may do it with joy, and not with grief: for that is unprofitable for you. *Hebrews 13:17*

Brethren, if a man be overtaken in a fault, ye which are spiritual, restore such an one in the spirit of meekness; considering thyself, lest thou also be tempted. *Galatians 6:1*

Moreover if thy brother shall trespass against thee, go and tell him his fault between thee and him alone: if he shall hear thee, thou hast gained thy brother. But if he will not hear thee, then take with thee one or two more, that in the mouth of two or three witnesses every word may be established. And if he shall neglect to hear them, tell it unto the church: but if he neglect to hear the church, let him be unto thee as an heathen man and a publican. *Matthew 18:15-17*

How is it then, brethren? when ye come together, every one of you hath a psalm, hath a doctrine, hath a tongue, hath a revelation, hath an interpretation. Let all things be done unto edifying.

For God is not the author of confusion, but of peace, as in all churches of the saints.

1 Corinthians 14:26,33

GOD'S COVENANT WORD
CONCERNING:

WORK

Servants, be obedient to them that are your masters according to the flesh, with fear and trembling, in singleness of your heart, as unto Christ;

Not with eyeservice, as menpleasers; but as the servants of Christ, doing the will of God from the heart;

With good will doing service, as to the Lord, and not to men:

Knowing that whatsoever good thing any man doeth, the same shall he receive of the Lord, whether he be bond or free. *Ephesians 6:5-8*

Do all things without murmurings and disputings.
Philippians 2:14

Servants, be subject to your masters with all fear; not only to the good and gentle, but also to the froward.

For this is thankworthy, if a man for conscience toward God endure grief, suffering wrongfully.

1 Peter 2:18,19

Commit thy works unto the Lord, and thy thoughts shall be established. *Proverbs 16:3*

Let every man prove his own work, and then shall he have rejoicing in himself alone, and not in another. *Galatians 6:4*

...Study to be quiet, and to do your own business, and to work with your own hands, as we commanded you;

That ye may walk honestly toward them that are without, and that ye may have lack of nothing.

1 Thessalonians 4:11,12

He that tilleth his land shall have plenty of bread: but he that followeth after vain persons shall have poverty enough.   *Proverbs 28:19*

He becometh poor that dealeth with a slack hand: but the hand of the diligent maketh rich.
                                        Proverbs 10:4

I know thy works: behold, I have set before thee an open door, and no man can shut it: for thou hast a little strength, and hast kept my word, and hast not denied my name.   *Revelation 3:8*

GOD'S COVENANT WORD
CONCERNING:

POLITICS

Blessed is the nation whose God is the Lord: and the people whom he hath chosen for his own inheritance. *Psalm 33:12*

Righteousness exalteth a nation: but sin is a reproach to any people. *Proverbs 14:34*

The Lord knoweth how to deliver the godly out of temptations, and to reserve the unjust unto the day of judgment to be punished:

But chiefly them that walk after the flesh in the lust of uncleanness, and despise government. Presumptuous are they, selfwilled, they are not afraid to speak evil of dignities.

Whereas angels, which are greater in power and might, bring not railing accusation against them before the Lord. *2 Peter 2:9-11*

Let every soul be subject unto the higher powers. For there is no power but of God: the powers that be are ordained of God.

Whosoever therefore resisteth the power, resisteth the ordinance of God.   *Romans 13:1,2*

At what instant I shall speak concerning a nation, and concerning a kingdom, to pluck up, and to pull down, and to destroy it; If that nation, against whom I have pronounced, turn from their evil, I will repent of the evil that I thought to do unto them.   *Jeremiah 18:7,8*

Submit yourselves to every ordinance of man for the Lord's sake: whether it be to the king, as supreme;

Or unto governors, as unto them that are sent by him for the punishment of evildoers, and for the praise of them that do well.

Honour all men. Love the brotherhood. Fear God. Honour the king.   *1 Peter 2:13,14,17*

GOD'S COVENANT WORD
CONCERNING:

FRIENDS

A man that hath friends must shew himself friendly: and there is a friend that sticketh closer than a brother. *Proverbs 18:24*

A friend loveth at all times, and a brother is born for adversity. *Proverbs 17:17*

This is my commandment, That ye love one another, as I have loved you. Greater love hath no man than this, that a man lay down his life for his friends. *John 15:12,13*

A new commandment I give unto you, That ye love one another; as I have loved you, that ye also love one another. By this shall all men know that ye are my disciples, if ye have love one to another. *John 13:34,35*

If there be therefore any consolation in Christ, if any comfort of love, if any fellowship of the Spirit, if any bowels and mercies,

Fulfil ye my joy, that ye be likeminded, having the same love, being of one accord, of one mind.

Let nothing be done through strife or vainglory; but in lowliness of mind let each esteem other better than themselves.

Look not every man on his own things, but every man also on the things of others.

Philippians 2:1-4

He that walketh with wise men shall be wise: but a companion of fools shall be destroyed.

Proverbs 13:20

We took sweet counsel together, and walked unto the house of God in company. *Psalm 55:14*

GOD'S COVENANT WORD
CONCERNING:

ENEMIES

When a man's ways please the Lord, he maketh even his enemies to be at peace with him.

Proverbs 16:7

Rejoice not when thine enemy falleth, and let not thine heart be glad when he stumbleth:

Lest the Lord see it, and it displease him, and he turn away his wrath from him. *Proverbs 24:17,18*

But I say unto you, Love your enemies, bless them that curse you, do good to them that hate you, and pray for them which despitefully use you, and persecute you; That ye may be the children of your Father which is in heaven: for he maketh his sun to rise on the evil and on the good, and sendeth rain on the just and on the unjust. For if ye love them which love you, what reward have ye? *Matthew 5:44-46*

Then said Jesus, Father, forgive them; for they know not what they do. *Luke 23:34*

Bless them which persecute you: bless, and curse not.

Dearly beloved, avenge not yourselves, but rather give place unto wrath: for it is written, Vengeance is mine; I will repay, saith the Lord.

Therefore if thine enemy hunger, feed him; if he thirst, give him drink: for in so doing thou shalt heap coals of fire on his head.

Romans 12:14,19,20

What shall we then say to these things? If God be for us, who can be against us? *Romans 8:31*

It is God that avengeth me, and subdueth the people under me.

He delivereth me from mine enemies: yea, thou liftest me up above those that rise up against me: thou hast delivered me from the violent man.

Psalm 18:47,48

GOD'S COVENANT WORD
CONCERNING:

NEIGHBORS

And he [a lawyer] answering said, Thou shalt love the Lord thy God with all thy heart, and with all thy soul, and with all thy strength, and with all thy mind; and thy neighbour as thyself. And he [Jesus] said unto him, Thou hast answered right: this do, and thou shalt live.   *Luke 10:27,28*

If ye fulfil the royal law according to the scripture, Thou shalt love thy neighbour as thyself, ye do well.   *James 2:8*

Debate thy cause with thy neighbor himself; and discover not a secret to another.   *Proverbs 25:9*

Thou shalt not defraud thy neighbor, neither rob him:....

Thou shalt not avenge, nor bear any grudge

against the children of thy people, but thou shalt love thy neighbour as thyself: I am the Lord.

Leviticus 19:13,18

Lord, who shall abide in thy tabernacle? who shall dwell in thy holy hill?

He that walketh uprightly, and worketh righteousness, and speaketh the truth in his heart.

He that backbiteth not with his tongue, nor doeth evil to his neighbour, nor taketh up a reproach against his neighbour. *Psalm 15:1-3*

Say not unto thy neighbour, Go, and come again, and to morrow I will give; when thou hast it by thee.

Devise not evil against thy neighbour, seeing he dwelleth securely by thee. *Proverbs 3:28,29*

Love worketh no ill to his neighbour: therefore love is the fulfilling of the law. *Romans 13:10*

For all the law is fulfilled in one word, even in this; Thou shalt love thy neighbour as thyself.

Galatians 5:14

GOD'S COVENANT WARNINGS
CONCERNING:

PREJUDICE

For by one Spirit are we all baptized into one body, whether we be Jews or Gentiles, whether we be bond or free; and have been all made to drink into one Spirit.

But now hath God set the members every one of them in the body, as it hath pleased him.

And those members of the body, which we think to be less honourable, upon these we bestow more abundant honour....

That there should be no schism in the body; but that the members should have the same care one for another.   *1 Corinthians 12:13,18,23,25*

There is neither Jew nor Greek, there is neither bond nor free, there is neither male nor female: for ye are all one in Christ Jesus.
Galatians 3:28

And Miriam and Aaron spake against Moses because of the Ethiopian woman whom he had married: for he had married an Ethiopian woman.... And the anger of the Lord was kindled against them.... And, behold, Miriam became leprous, white as snow: and Aaron looked upon Miriam, and, behold, she was leprous. And Aaron said unto Moses, Alas, my lord, I beseech thee, lay not the sin upon us, wherein we have done foolishly, and wherein we have sinned.   *Numbers 12:1,9-11*

If there come unto your assembly a man with a gold ring, in goodly apparel, and there come in also a poor man in vile raiment;

And ye have respect to him that weareth the gay clothing, and say unto him, Sit thou here in a good place; and say to the poor, Stand thou there, or sit here under my footstool:

Are ye not then partial in yourselves, and are become judges of evil thoughts?

But if ye have respect to persons, ye commit sin, and are convinced of the law as transgressors.

James 2:2-4,9

God's Covenant Warnings
Concerning:

Gossip

Speak not evil one of another.   *James 4:11*

Thou shalt not go up and down as a talebearer among thy people.   *Leviticus 19:16*

A talebearer revealeth secrets: but he that is of a faithful spirit concealeth the matter.

Proverbs 11:13

He that covereth a transgression seeketh love; but he that repeateth a matter separateth very friends.   *Proverbs 17:9*

If any man among you seem to be religious, and bridleth not his tongue, but deceiveth his own heart, this man's religion is vain.   *James 1:26*

For he that will love life, and see good days, let him refrain his tongue from evil, and his lips that they speak no guile. *1 Peter 3:10*

Where no wood is, there the fire goeth out: so where there is no talebearer, the strife ceaseth.

As coals are to burning coals, and wood to fire; so is a contentious man to kindle strife.

The words of a talebearer are as wounds, and they go down into the innermost parts of the belly. *Proverbs 26:20-22*

Let no corrupt communication proceed out of your mouth, but that which is good to the use of edifying, that it may minister grace unto the hearers.

And grieve not the holy Spirit of God, whereby ye are sealed unto the day of redemption.

Let all bitterness, and wrath, and anger, and clamour, and evil speaking, be put away from you, with all malice:

And be ye kind one to another, tenderhearted, forgiving one another, even as God for Christ's sake hath forgiven you. *Ephesians 4:29-32*

GOD'S COVENANT WARNINGS
CONCERNING:

LYING

Remove from me the way of lying: and grant me thy law graciously. *Psalm 119:29*

Lie not one to another, seeing that ye have put off the old man with his deeds. *Colossians 3:9*

...Put on the new man, which after God is created in righteousness and true holiness.

Wherefore putting away lying, speak every man truth with his neigbour. *Ephesians 4:24,25*

A righteous man hateth lying: but a wicked man is loathsome, and cometh to shame. *Proverbs 13:5*

He that worketh deceit shall not dwell within my house: he that telleth lies shall not tarry in my sight. *Psalm 101:7*

These six things doth the Lord hate: yea, seven are an abomination unto him: A proud look, a lying tongue, and hands that shed innocent blood, An heart the deviseth wicked imaginations, feet that be swift in running to mischief,

A false witness that speaketh lies, and he that soweth discord among brethren. *Proverbs 6:16-19*

Peter said, Ananias, why hath Satan filled thine heart to lie to the Holy Ghost, and to keep back part of the price of the land? Whiles it remained, was it not thine own? and after it was sold, was it not in thine own power? why hast thou conceived this thing in thine heart? thou hast not lied unto men, but unto God. *Acts 5:3,4*

Deliver my soul, O Lord, from lying lips, and from a deceitful tongue. *Psalm 120:2*

GOD'S COVENANT WARNINGS
CONCERNING:

VENGEANCE

Dearly beloved, avenge not yourselves, but rather give place unto wrath: for it is written, Vengeance is mine; I will repay, saith the Lord.

Romans 12:19

Thou shalt not avenge, nor bear any grudge against the children of thy people, but thou shalt love thy neighbour as thyself.   *Leviticus 19:18*

A soft answer turneth away wrath: but grievous words stir up anger.   *Proverbs 15:1*

Having a good conscience; that, whereas they speak evil of you, as of evildoers, they may be ashamed that falsely accuse your good conversation in Christ.

For it is better, if the will of God be so, that ye suffer for well doing, than for evil doing.

1 Peter 3:16,17

Ye have heard that it hath been said, An eye for an eye, and a tooth for a tooth: But I say unto you, That ye resist not evil: but whosoever shall smite thee on thy right cheek, turn to him the other also. And if any man will sue thee at the law, and take away thy coat, let him have thy cloak also. And whosoever shall compel thee to go a mile, go with him twain. Give to him that asketh thee, and from him that would borrow of thee turn not thou away.

Ye have heard that it hath been said, Thou shalt love thy neighbour, and hate thine enemy. But I say unto you, Love your enemies, bless them that curse you, do good to them that hate you, and pray for them which despitefully use you, and persecute you; That ye may be the children of your Father which is in heaven.

Matthew 5:38-45

GOD'S COVENANT WARNINGS
CONCERNING:

LUST

Dearly beloved, I beseech you as strangers and pilgrims, abstain from fleshly lusts, which war against the soul.   *1 Peter 2:11*

That he no longer should live the rest of his time in the flesh to the lusts of men, but to the will of God.   *1 Peter 4:2*

Among whom also we all had our conversation in times past in the lusts of our flesh, fulfilling the desires of the flesh and of the mind; and were by nature the children of wrath, even as others.

Ephesians 2:3

All that is in the world, the lust of the flesh, and the lust of the eyes, and the pride of life, is not of the Father, but is of the world.

And the world passeth away, and the lust thereof: but he that doeth the will of God abideth for ever. *1 John 2:16,17*

Flee also youthful lusts. *2 Timothy 2:22*

But every man is tempted, when he is drawn away of his own lust, and enticed.

Then when lust hath conceived, it bringeth forth sin: and sin, when it is finished, bringeth forth death. *James 1:14,15*

Let not sin therefore reign in your mortal body, that ye should obey it in the lusts thereof. *Romans 6:12*

This I say then, Walk in the Spirit, and ye shall not fulfil the lust of the flesh.

For the flesh lusteth against the Spirit, and the Spirit against the flesh: and these are contrary the one to the other: so that ye cannot do the things that ye would. *Galatians 5:16,17*

But put ye on the Lord Jesus Christ, and make not provision for the flesh, to fulfil the lusts thereof. *Romans 13:14*

God's Covenant Warnings
Concerning:

Adultery and Fornication

Now the works of the flesh are manifest, which are these; Adultery, fornication, uncleanness, lasciviousness. *Galatians 5:19*

Thou shalt not commit adultery. *Exodus 20:14*

But fornication, and all uncleanness, or covetousness, let it not be once named among you, as becometh saints;

For this ye know, that no whoremonger, nor unclean person, nor covetous man, who is an idolater, hath any inheritance in the kingdom of Christ and of God. *Ephesians 5:3,5*

But whoso committeth adultery with a woman lacketh understanding: he that doeth it destroyeth his own soul. A wound and dishonour shall he get; and his reproach shall not be wiped away.

Proverbs 6:32,33

Ye adulterers and adulteresses, know ye not that the friendship of the world is enmity with God? whosoever therefore will be a friend of the world is the enemy of God. *James 4:4*

Nevertheless, to avoid fornication, let every man have his own wife, and let every woman have her own husband. *1 Corinthians 7:2*

Marriage is honorable in all, and the bed undefiled. *Hebrews 13:4*

Know ye not that your bodies are the members of Christ? shall I then take the members of Christ, and make them the members of an harlot? God forbid.

What? know ye not that he which is joined to an harlot is one body? for two, saith he, shall be one flesh.

But he that is joined unto the Lord is one spirit.

Flee fornication. Every sin that a man doeth is without the body; but he that committeth fornication sinneth against his own body.

What? know ye not that your body is the temple of the Holy Ghost which is in you, which ye have of God, and ye are not your own?

For ye are bought with a price:....

1 Corinthians 6:15-20

GOD'S COVENANT WARNINGS

CONCERNING:

SEXUAL PERVERSION

Know ye not that the unrighteous shall not inherit the kingdom of God? Be not deceived: neither fornicators, nor idolaters, nor adulterers, nor effeminate, nor abusers of themselves with mankind,

Nor thieves, nor covetous, nor drunkards, nor revilers, nor extortioners, shall inherit the kingdom of God.   *1 Corinthians 6:9,10*

Professing themselves to be wise, they became fools,

Wherefore God also gave them up to uncleanness through the lusts of their own hearts, to dishonour their own bodies between themselves:

Who changed the truth of God into a lie, and worshipped and served the creature more than the Creator, who is blessed for ever. Amen.

For this cause God gave them up unto vile

affections: for even their women did change the natural use into that which is against nature:

And likewise also the men, leaving the natural use of the woman, burned in their lust one toward another; men with men working that which is unseemly, and receiving in themselves that recompence of their error which was meet.

And even as they did not like to retain God in their knowledge, God gave them over to a reprobate mind. *Romans 1:22,24-28*

Set your affection on things above, not on things on the earth.

Mortify therefore your members which are upon the earth; fornication, uncleanness, inordinate affection, evil concupiscence, and covetousness, which is idolatry. *Colossians 3:2,5*

For this is the will of God, even your sanctification, that ye should abstain from fornication:

That every one of you should know how to possess his vessel in sanctification and honour.

1 Thessalonians 4:3,4

COVENANT COMMANDMENTS
ON:

SEPARATION FROM THE WORLD

Love not the world, neither the things that are in the world. If any man love the world, the love of the Father is not in him.

For all that is in the world, the lust of the flesh, and the lust of the eyes, and the pride of life, is not of the Father, but is of the world.

And the world passeth away, and the lust thereof: but he that doeth the will of God abideth for ever. *I John 2:15-17*

Ye adulterers and adulteresses, know ye not that the friendship of the world is enmity with God? whosoever therefore will be a friend of the world is the enemy of God. *James 4:4*

For what is a man profited, if he shall gain the whole world, and lose his own soul? or what shall a man give in exchange for his soul?

Matthew 16:26

If ye were of the world, the world would love his own: but because ye are not of the world, but I have chosen you out of the world, therefore the world hateth you.

John 15:19

Set your affection on things above, not on things on the earth.

Colossians 3:2

No man that warreth entangleth himself with the affairs of this life; that he may please him who hath chosen him to be a soldier.

If we suffer, we shall also reign with him: if we deny him, he also will deny us.

2 Timothy 2:4,12

And be not conformed to this world: but be ye transformed by the renewing of your mind, that ye may prove what is that good, and acceptable, and perfect, will of God.

Romans 12:2

PART 4

GOD'S
COVENANT BLESSINGS
FOR SUCCESSFUL
CHRISTIAN LIVING

GOD'S COVENANT TRUTH
CONCERNING:

ACCEPTING MYSELF

The second [commandment] is like, namely this, Thou shalt love thy neighbor as thyself. There is none other commandment greater than these. *Mark 12:31*

To the praise of the glory of his grace, wherein he hath made us accepted in the beloved.

Ephesians 1:6

The Lord seeth not as man seeth; for man looketh on the outward appearance, but the Lord looketh on the heart. *1 Samuel 16:7*

So God created man in his own image, in the image of God created he him; male and female created he them. And God blessed them, and God said unto them, Be fruitful, and multiply, and replenish the earth, and subdue it: and have dominion over the fish of the sea, and over the fowl of the air, and over every living thing that moveth upon the earth. *Genesis 1:27,28*

But God, who is rich in mercy, for his great love wherewith he loved us,

Even when we were dead in sins, hath quickened us together with Christ, (by grace ye are saved;)

And hath raised us up together, and made us sit together in heavenly places in Christ Jesus.

Ephesians 2:4-6

Therefore if any man be in Christ, he is a new creature: old things are passed away; behold, all things are become new.

For he [God] hath made him [Jesus] to be sin for us, who knew no sin; that we might be made the righteousness of God in him.

2 Corinthians 5:17,21

There is therefore now no condemnation to them which are in Christ Jesus, who walk not after the flesh, but after the Spirit. *Romans 8:1*

I can do all things through Christ which strengtheneth me. *Philippians 4:13*

GOD'S COVENANT TRUTH
CONCERNING:

WHAT I THINK

Commit thy works unto the Lord, and thy thoughts shall be established.   *Proverbs 16:3*

And thou, Solomon my son, know thou the God of thy father, and serve him with a perfect heart and with a willing mind: for the Lord searcheth all hearts, and understandeth all the imaginations of the thoughts.   *1 Chronicles 28:9*

My son, forget not my law; but let thine heart keep my commandments: For length of days, and long life, and peace, shall they add to thee. Let not mercy and truth forsake thee: bind them about thy neck; write them upon the table of thine heart: So shalt thou find favour and good understanding in the sight of God and man.

Trust in the Lord with all thine heart; and lean not unto thine own understanding.

Proverbs 3:1-5

Thou wilt keep him in perfect peace, whose mind is stayed on thee: because he trusteth in thee.

Isaiah 26:3

For this is the covenant that I will make with the house of Israel after those days, saith the Lord; I will put my laws into their mind, and write them in their hearts: and I will be to them a God, and they shall be to me a people.

Hebrews 8:10

And be not conformed to this world: but be ye transformed by the renewing of your mind, that ye may prove what is that good, and acceptable, and perfect, will of God.   *Romans 12:2*

Finally, brethren, whatsoever things are true, whatsoever things are honest, whatsoever things are just, whatsoever things are pure, whatsoever things are lovely, whatsoever thing are of good report; if there be any virtue, and if there be any praise, think on these things.   *Philippians 4:8*

GOD'S COVENANT TRUTH
CONCERNING:

THE WORDS I SAY

Pleasant words are as an honeycomb, sweet to the soul, and health to the bones.

Proverbs 16:24

A soft answer turneth away wrath: but grievous words stir up anger. *Proverbs 15:1*

Let your speech be alway with grace, seasoned with salt, that ye may know how ye ought to answer every man. *Colossians 4:6*

Out of the abundance of the heart the mouth speaketh.... For by thy words thou shalt be justified, and by thy words thou shalt be condemned.

Matthew 12:34,37

Death and life are in the power of the tongue: and they that love it shall eat the fruit thereof.

Proverbs 18:21

Thou art snared with the words of thy mouth, thou art taken with the words of thy mouth.

Proverbs 6:2

As for me, this is my covenant with them, saith the Lord; My spirit that is upon thee, and my words which I have put in thy mouth, shall not depart out of thy mouth, nor out of the mouth of thy seed, nor out of the mouth of thy seed's seed, saith the Lord, from henceforth and for ever.

Isaiah 59:21

And Jesus answering saith unto them, Have faith in God. For verily I say unto you, That whosoever shall say unto this mountain, Be thou removed, and be thou cast into the sea; and shall not doubt in his heart, but shall believe that those things which he saith shall come to pass; he shall have whatsoever he saith.   *Mark 11:22,23*

GOD'S COVENANT TRUTH
CONCERNING:

SPIRITUAL WARFARE

Be sober, be vigilant; because your adversary the devil, as a roaring lion, walketh about, seeking whom he may devour:

Whom resist stedfast in the faith....

1 Peter 5:8,9

For we wrestle not against flesh and blood, but against principalities, against powers, against the rulers of the darkness of this world, against spiritual wickedness in high places. *Ephesians 6:12*

For though we walk in the flesh, we do not war after the flesh:

(For the weapons of our warfare are not carnal, but mighty through God to the pulling down of strong holds.) *2 Corinthians 10:3,4*

Fight the good fight of faith, lay hold on eternal life, whereunto thou art also called. *1 Timothy 6:12*

Who through faith subdued kingdoms, wrought righteousness, obtained promises, stopped the mouths of lions,

Quenched the violence of fire, escaped the edge of the sword, out of weakness were made strong, waxed valiant in fight, turned to flight the armies of the aliens. *Hebrews 11:33,34*

Behold, they shall surely gather together, but not by me: whosoever shall gather together against thee shall fall for thy sake. *Isaiah 54:15*

A thousand shall fall at thy side, and ten thousand at thy right hand; but it shall not come nigh thee. *Psalm 91:7*

Submit yourselves therefore to God. Resist the devil, and he will flee from you.

Draw nigh to God, and he will draw nigh to you.... *James 4:7,8*

GOD'S COVENANT TRUTH
CONCERNING:

THE BELIEVER'S AUTHORITY

What is man, that thou art mindful of him?....
Thou madest him to have dominion over the works of thy hands: thou hast put all things under his feet. *Psalm 8:4,6*

As the Father hath life in himself; so hath he given to the Son to have life in himself;
And hath given him authority to execute judgment also, because he is the Son of man.
John 5:26,27

Having spoiled principalities and powers, he [Jesus] made a shew of them openly, triumphing over them in it. *Colossians 2:15*

I am he that liveth, and was dead; and, behold,

I am alive for evermore, Amen; and have the keys of hell and of death. *Revelation 1:18*

I say also unto thee, That thou art Peter, and upon this rock I will build my church; and the gates of hell shall not prevail against it. And I will give unto thee the keys of the kingdom of heaven: and whatsoever thou shalt bind on earth shall be bound in heaven: and whatsoever thou shalt loose on earth shall be loosed in heaven.

Matthew 16:18,19

He called his twelve disciples together, and gave them power and authority over all devils, and to cure diseases. *Luke 9:1*

Behold, I give unto you power to tread on serpents and scorpions, and over all the power of the enemy: and nothing shall by any means hurt you. *Luke 10:19*

The God of peace shall bruise Satan under your feet shortly. *Romans 16:20*

GOD'S COVENANT TRUTH
CONCERNING:

WEAPONS OF OUR WARFARE

Take the helmet of salvation, and the sword of the Spirit, which is the word of God.

Ephesians 6:17

So shall my word be that goeth forth out of my mouth: it shall not return unto me void, but it shall accomplish that which I please, and it shall prosper in the thing whereto I sent it.   *Isaiah 55:11*

I have written unto you, fathers, because ye have know him that is from the beginning. I have written unto you, young men, because ye are strong, and the word of God abideth in you, and ye have overcome the wicked one.   *1 John 2:14*

And they overcame him by the blood of the Lamb, and by the word of their testimony; and they loved not their lives unto the death.

Revelation 12:11

Who hath delivered us from the power of darkness, and hath translated us into the kingdom of his dear Son:

In whom we have redemption through his blood, even the forgiveness of sins.

Colossians 1:13,14

Wherefore God also hath highly exalted him, and given him a name which is above every name:

That at the name of Jesus every knee should bow, of things in heaven, and things in earth, and things under the earth;

And that every tongue should confess that Jesus Christ is Lord, to the glory of God the Father.

Philippians 2:9-11

And these signs shall follow them that believe; In my name shall they cast out devils.... *Mark 16:17*

The weapons of our warfare are not carnal, but mighty through God to the pulling down of strong holds. *2 Corinthians 10:4*

GOD'S COVENANT TRUTH
CONCERNING:

CHRISTIAN MATURITY

For the perfecting of the saints, for the work of the ministry, for the edifying of the body of Christ:

Till we all come in the unity of the faith, and of the knowledge of the Son of God, unto a perfect man, unto the measure of the stature of the fulness of Christ:

That we henceforth be no more children, tossed to and fro, and carried about with every wind of doctrine, by the sleight of men, and cunning craftiness, whereby they lie in wait to deceive;

But speaking the truth in love, may grow up into him in all things, which is the head, even Christ:

From whom the whole body fitly joined together and compacted by that which every joint supplieth, according to the effectual working in the measure of every part, maketh increase of the body unto the edifying of itself in love.   *Ephesians 4:12-16*

Therefore leaving the principles of the doctrine of Christ, let us go on unto perfection; not laying again the foundation of repentance from dead works, and of faith toward God.

Hebrews 6:1

Be ye therefore perfect, even as your Father which is in heaven is perfect. *Matthew 5:48*

Now the God of peace, that brought again from the dead our Lord Jesus, that great shepherd of the sheep, through the blood of the everlasting covenant,

Make you perfect in every good work to do his will, working in you that which is wellpleasing in his sight, through Jesus Christ; to whom be glory for ever and ever. Amen. *Hebrews 13:20,21*

God's Covenant Truth
Concerning:

Faithfulness

A faithful man shall abound with blessings.

Proverbs 28:20

He that is faithful in that which is least is faithful also in much:.... And if ye have not been faithful in that which is another man's, who shall give you that which is your own? *Luke 16:10,12*

Fear none of those things which thou shalt suffer: behold, the devil shall cast some of you into prison, that ye may be tried; and ye shall have tribulation ten days; be thou faithful unto death, and I will give thee a crown of life.

Revelation 2:10

And let us not be weary in well doing: for in due season we shall reap, if we faint not. *Galatians 6:9*

That ye might walk worthy of the Lord unto all pleasing, being fruitful in every good work, and increasing in the knowledge of God;

If ye continue in the faith grounded and settled, and be not moved away from the hope of the gospel, which ye have heard, and which was preached to every creature which is under heaven.

Colossians 1:10,23

His lord said unto him, Well done, thou good and faithful servant: thou hast been faithful over a few things, I will make thee ruler over many things: enter thou into the joy of thy lord.

Matthew 25:21

I thank Christ Jesus our Lord, who hath enabled me, for that he counted me faithful, putting me into the ministry. *1 Timothy 1:12*

The things that thou hast heard of me among many witnesses, the same commit thou to faithful men, who shall be able to teach others also.

2 Timothy 2:2

GOD'S COVENANT TRUTH
CONCERNING:

BELIEVER'S HOLINESS AND PURITY

As he which hath called you is holy, so be ye holy in all manner of conversation;
Because it is written, Be ye holy; for I am holy.

1 Peter 1:15,16

According as he hath chosen us in him before the foundation of the world, that we should be holy and without blame before him in love.

Ephesians 1:4

Who gave himself for us, that he might redeem us from all iniquity, and purify unto himself a peculiar people, zealous of good works.

Titus 2:14

What? know ye not that your body is the temple of the Holy Ghost which is in you, which ye have of God, and ye are not your own?

For ye are bought with a price: therefore glorify God in your body, and in your spirit, which are God's.   *1 Corinthians 6:19,20*

I beseech you therefore, brethren, by the mercies of God, that ye present your bodies a living sacrifice, holy, acceptable unto God, which is your reasonable service.

And be not conformed to this world: but be ye transformed by the renewing of your mind, that ye may prove what is that good, and acceptable, and perfect, will of God.   *Romans 12:1,2*

If a man therefore purge himself from these, he shall be a vessel unto honour, sanctified, and meet for the master's use, and prepared unto every good work.   *2 Timothy 2:21*

Who shall ascend into the hill of the Lord? or who shall stand in his holy place?

He that hath clean hands, and a pure heart; who hath not lifted up his soul unto vanity, nor sworn deceitfully.

He shall receive the blessing from the Lord, and righteousness from the God of his salvation.

Psalm 24:3-5

GOD'S COVENANT TRUTH
CONCERNING:

BELIEVER'S INTEGRITY

The just man walketh in his integrity: his children are blessed after him.   *Proverbs 20:7*

That which is altogether just shalt thou follow, that thou mayest live, and inherit the land which the Lord thy God giveth thee.

Deuteronomy 16:20

The integrity of the upright shall guide them: but the perverseness of transgressors shall destroy them.   *Proverbs 11:3*

So he [David] fed them [the Israelites] according to the integrity of his heart; and guided them by the skilfulness of his hands.

Psalm 78:72

The Lord shall judge the people: judge me, O Lord, according to my righteousness, and according to mine integrity that is in me.   *Psalm 7:8*

Let me be weighed in an even balance that God may know mine integrity.   *Job 31:6*

Let integrity and uprightness preserve me; for I wait on thee.   *Psalm 25:21*

And herein do I exercise myself, to have always a conscience void of offence toward God, and toward men.   *Acts 24:16*

And as for me, thou upholdest me in mine integrity, and settest me before thy face for ever.   *Psalm 41:12*

Judge me, O Lord; for I have walked in mine integrity: I have trusted also in the Lord; therefore I shall not slide.   *Psalm 26:1*

But as for me, I will walk in mine integrity: redeem me, and be merciful unto me.

Psalm 26:11

GOD'S COVENANT TRUTH
CONCERNING:

COVENANT HONESTY

We beseech you, brethren, that ye increase more and more;

And that ye study to be quiet, and to do your own business, and to work with your own hands, as we commanded you;

That ye may walk honestly toward them that are without, and that ye may have lack of nothing.

1 Thessalonians 4:10-12

These are the things that ye shall do; Speak ye every man the truth to his neighbour; execute the judgment of truth and peace in your gates.

Zechariah 8:16

Let not mercy and truth forsake thee: bind them about thy neck; write them upon the table of thine heart.

Proverbs 3:3

I have chosen the way of truth: thy judgments have I laid before me. *Psalm 119:30*

Wherefore putting away lying, speak every man truth with his neighbour: for we are members one of another. *Ephesians 4:25*

But have renounced the hidden things of dishonesty, not walking in craftiness, nor handling the word of God deceitfully; but by manifestation of the truth commending ourselves to every man's conscience in the sight of God. *2 Corinthians 4:2*

Teach me thy way, O Lord; I will walk in thy truth: unite my heart to fear thy name. *Psalm 86:11*

And said, Remember now, O Lord, I beseech thee, how I have walked before thee in truth and with a perfect heart, and have done that which is good in thy sight. *Isaiah 38:3*

I have no greater joy than to hear that my children walk in truth. *3 John 4*

God's Covenant Truth
Concerning:

Covenant Commitment

Jesus said unto him, Thou shalt love the Lord thy God with all thy heart, and with all thy soul, and with all thy mind.   *Matthew 22:37*

Submit yourselves therefore to God. *James 4:7*

Now be ye not stiffnecked, as your fathers were, but yield yourselves unto the Lord...and serve the Lord your God....   *2 Chronicles 30:8*

Moses had said, Consecrate yourselves to day to the Lord.   *Exodus 32:29*

Neither yield ye your members as instruments of unrighteousness unto sin: but yield yourselves unto God, as those that are alive from the dead, and your members as instruments of righteousness unto God.   *Romans 6:13*

I beseech you therefore, brethren, by the mercies of God, that ye present your bodies a living sacrifice, holy, acceptable unto God, which is your reasonable service.

And be not conformed to this world: but be ye transformed by the renewing of your mind, that ye may prove what is that good, and acceptable, and perfect, will of God.   *Romans 12:1,2*

For the which cause I also suffer these things: nevertheless I am not ashamed: for I know whom I have believed, and am persuaded that he is able to keep that which I have committed unto him against that day.   *2 Timothy 1:12*

His lord said unto him, Well done, thou good and faithful servant: thou hast been faithful over a few things, I will make thee ruler over many things: enter thou into the joy of thy Lord.

Matthew 25:21

GOD'S COVENANT TRUTH
CONCERNING:

COVENANT REST

Come unto me, all ye that labour and are heavy laden, and I will give you rest. Take my yoke upon you, and learn of me; for I am meek and lowly in heart: and ye shall find rest unto your souls.

Matthew 11:28,29

Harden not your hearts, as in the provocation, in the day of temptation in the wilderness:

When your fathers tempted me, proved me, and saw my works forty years.

Let us therefore fear, lest, a promise being left us of entering into his rest, any of you should seem to come short of it.

For unto us was the gospel preached, as well as unto them: but the word preached did not profit them, not being mixed with faith in them that heard it.

For we which have believed do enter into rest.
Hebrews 3:8,9;4:1-3

There remaineth therefore a rest to the people of God.

For he that is entered into his rest, he also hath ceased from his own works, as God did from his.

Let us labour therefore to enter into that rest, lest any man fall after the same example of unbelief.
Hebrews 4:9-11

Return unto thy rest, O my soul; for the Lord hath dealt bountifully with thee.   *Psalm 116:7*

In returning and rest shall ye be saved; in quietness and in confidence shall be your strength.
Isaiah 30:15

Rest in the Lord, and wait patiently for him.
Psalm 37:7

Thus saith the Lord, Stand ye in the ways, and see, and ask for the old paths, where is the good

way, and walk therein, and ye shall find rest for
your souls.   *Jeremiah 6:16*

God's Covenant Truth
Concerning:

Covenant Steadfastness

Therefore, my beloved brethren, be ye stedfast, unmoveable, always abounding in the work of the Lord, forasmuch as ye know that your labour is not in vain in the Lord.   *1 Corinthians 15:58*

For now we live, if ye stand fast in the Lord.

To the end he may stablish your hearts unblameable in holiness before God, even our Father, at the coming of our Lord Jesus Christ with all his saints.   *1 Thessalonians 3:8,13*

Therefore, brethren, stand fast, and hold the traditions which ye have been taught, whether by word, or our epistle.   *2 Thessalonians 2:15*

Stand fast therefore in the liberty wherewith Christ hath made us free, and be not entangled again with the yoke of bondage. *Galatians 5:1*

But let him ask in faith, nothing wavering. For he that wavereth is like a wave of the sea driven with the wind and tossed.

A double minded man is unstable in all his ways.
James 1:6,8

That we henceforth be no more children, tossed to and fro, and carried about with every wind of doctrine, by the sleight of men, and cunning craftiness, whereby they lie in wait to deceive.
Ephesians 4:14

Therefore, my brethren dearly beloved and longed for, my joy and crown, so stand fast in the Lord, my dearly beloved. *Philippians 4:1*

The Lord God will help me; therefore shall I not be confounded: therefore have I set my face like a flint, and I know that I shall not be ashamed.
Isaiah 50:7

GOD'S COVENANT TRUTH
CONCERNING:

COVENANT PRAYER

Be careful for nothing; but in every thing by prayer and supplication with thanksgiving let your requests be made known unto God.

Philippians 4:6

Pray without ceasing.

In every thing give thanks: for this is the will of God in Christ Jesus concerning you.

1 Thessalonians 5:17,18

And take the helmet of salvation, and the sword of the Spirit, which is the word of God:

Praying always with all prayer and supplication in the Spirit, and watching thereunto with all perseverance and supplication for all saints.

Ephesians 6:17,18

I will pray with the spirit, and I will pray with the understanding also: I will sing with the spirit, and I will sing with the understanding also.

1 Corinthians 14:15

If ye abide in me, and my words abide in you, ye shall ask what ye will, and it shall be done unto you. *John 15:7*

And this is the confidence that we have in him, that, if we ask any thing according to his will, he heareth us:

And if we know that he hear us, whatsoever we ask, we know that we have the petitions that we desired of him. *1 John 5:14,15*

Pray one for another, that ye may be healed. The effectual fervent prayer of a righteous man availeth much. *James 5:16*

If ye shall ask any thing in my name, I will do it.

John 14:14

Therefore I say unto you, What things soever ye desire, when ye pray, believe that ye receive them, and ye shall have them. *Mark 11:24*

God's Covenant Truth
Concerning:

Covenant Unity

Behold, how good and how pleasant it is for brethren to dwell together in unity! *Psalm 133:1*

That they all may be one; as thou, Father, art in me, and I in thee, that they also may be one in us: that the world may believe that thou hast sent me. And the glory which thou gavest me I have given them; that they may be one, even as we are one: I in them, and thou in me, that they may be made perfect in one; and that the world may know that thou hast sent me, and hast loved them, as thou hast loved me.   *John 17:21-23*

Now the God of patience and consolation grant you to be likeminded one toward another according to Christ Jesus:

That ye may with one mind and one mouth glorify God, even the Father of our Lord Jesus Christ.

Romans 15:5,6

Now I beseech you, brethren, by the name of our Lord Jesus Christ, that ye all speak the same thing, and that there be no divisions among you; but that ye be perfectly joined together in the same mind and in the same judgment.

1 Corinthians 1:10

Endeavouring to keep the unity of the Spirit in the bond of peace.

There is one body, and one Spirit, even as ye are called in one hope of your calling.

Ephesians 4:3,4

Only let your conversation be as it becometh the gospel of Christ: that whether I come and see you, or else be absent, I may hear of your affairs, that ye stand fast in one spirit, with one mind striving together for the faith of the gospel.

Philippians 1:27

Fulfil ye my joy, that ye be likeminded, having the same love, being of one accord, of one mind.

Philippians 2:2

PART 5

GOD'S
COVENANT BLESSINGS
FOR FINANCES

GOD'S COVENANT WORD ON:

PERSONAL FINANCES

My God shall supply all your need according to his riches in glory by Christ Jesus. *Philippians 4:19*

Therefore take no thought, saying, What shall we eat? or, What shall we drink? or, Wherewithal shall we be clothed? (For after all these things do the Gentiles seek:) for your heavenly Father knoweth that ye have need of all these things. But seek ye first the kingdom of God, and his righteousness; and all these things shall be added unto you. *Matthew 6:31-33*

This book of the law shall not depart out of thy mouth; but thou shalt meditate therein day and night, that thou mayest observe to do according to all that is written therein: for then thou shalt make thy way prosperous, and then thou shalt have good success. *Joshua 1:8*

Beloved, I wish above all things that thou mayest prosper and be in health, even as thy soul prospereth. *3 John 2*

For God giveth to a man that is good in his sight wisdom, and knowledge, and joy: but to the sinner he giveth travail, to gather and to heap up, that he may give to him that is good before God. *Ecclesiastes 2:26*

But thou shalt remember the Lord thy God: for it is he that giveth thee power to get wealth. *Deuteronomy 8:18*

If they [the righteous] obey and serve him [God], they shall spend their days in prosperity, and their years in pleasures. *Job 36:11*

Let the Lord be magnified, which hath pleasure in the prosperity of his servant. *Psalm 35:27*

Delight thyself also in the Lord; and he shall give thee the desires of thine heart. *Psalm 37:4*

GOD'S COVENANT WORD ON:

CHILDREN'S PROSPERITY

And all thy children shall be taught of the Lord; and great shall be the peace of thy children.
Isaiah 54:13

I have been young, and now am old; yet have I not seen the righteous forsaken, nor his seed begging bread.

He is ever merciful, and lendeth; and his seed is blessed. *Psalm 37:25,26*

The mercy of the Lord is from everlasting to everlasting upon them that fear him, and his righteousness unto children's children.

Psalm 103:17

The Lord shall increase you more and more, you and your children.

Ye are blessed of the Lord which made heaven and earth. *Psalm 115:14,15*

A good man leaveth an inheritance to his children's children: and the wealth of the sinner is laid up for the just.   *Proverbs 13:22*

The just man walketh in his integrity: his children are blessed after him.   *Proverbs 20:7*

Praise ye the Lord. Blessed is the man that feareth the Lord, that delighteth greatly in his commandments.

His seed shall be mighty upon earth: the generation of the upright shall be blessed.

Wealth and riches shall be in his house: and his righteousness endureth for ever.   *Psalm 112:1-3*

I will make an everlasting covenant with them. And their seed shall be known among the Gentiles, and their offspring among the people: all that see them shall acknowledge them, that they are the seed which the Lord hath blessed.

Isaiah 61:8,9

GOD'S COVENANT WORD ON:

GIVING

Give, and it shall be given unto you; good measure, pressed down, and shaken together, and running over, shall men give into your bosom. For with the same measure that ye mete withal it shall be measured to you again.   *Luke 6:38*

Bring ye all the tithes into the storehouse, that there may be meat in mine house, and prove me now herewith, saith the Lord of hosts, if I will not open you the windows of heaven, and pour you out a blessing, that there shall not be room enough to receive it.   *Malachi 3:10*

But this I say, He which soweth sparingly shall reap also sparingly; and he which soweth bountifully shall reap also bountifully.

Every man according as he purposeth in his heart, so let him give; not grudgingly, or of necessity: for

God loveth a cheerful giver. And God is able to make all grace abound toward you; that ye, always having all sufficiency in all things, may abound to every good work. *2 Corinthians 9:6-8*

Upon the first day of the week let every one of you lay by him in store, as God hath prospered him, that there be no gatherings when I come.
1 Corinthians 16:2

He [Jesus] called unto him his disciples, and saith unto them, Verily I say unto you, That this poor widow hath cast more in, than all they which have cast into the treasury: For all they did cast in of their abundance; but she of her want did cast in all that she had, even all her living.
Mark 12:43-44

Poverty and shame shall be to him that refuseth instruction: but he that regardeth reproof shall be honoured. *Proverbs 13:18*

God's Covenant Word on:

Debt-Free Living

The Lord shall open unto thee his good treasure, the heaven to give the rain unto thy land in his season, and to bless all the work of thine hand: and thou shalt lend unto many nations, and thou shalt not borrow. *Deuteronomy 28:12*

The borrower is servant to the lender.
Proverbs 22:7

The Lord thy God blesseth thee, as he promised thee: and thou shalt lend unto many nations, but thou shalt not borrow; and thou shalt reign over many nations, but they shall not reign over thee. *Deuteronomy 15:6*

There cried a certain woman ... saying, Thy servant my husband is dead;... and the creditor is come to take unto him my two sons to be bondmen. And Elisha said unto her, What shall I do for thee? tell me, what hast thou in the house? And she said,... not any thing... save a pot of oil. Then he said, Go, borrow thee vessels abroad of all thy neighbours, even empty vessels; borrow not a few. And when thou art come in,... pour out into all those vessels.... And it came to pass, when the vessels were full.... She came and told the man of God. And he said, Go, sell the oil, and pay thy debt, and live thou and thy children of the rest.   *2 Kings 4:1-4,6,7*

Give to him that asketh thee, and from him that would borrow of thee turn not thou away.
Matthew 5:42

The wicked borroweth, and payeth not again: but the righteous sheweth mercy, and giveth.
Psalm 37:21

Better is it that thou shouldest not vow, than that thou shouldest vow and not pay.
Ecclesiastes 5:5

GOD'S COVENANT WORD ON:

HIS ATTITUDE TOWARD THE POOR

Blessed is he that considereth the poor: the Lord will deliver him in time of trouble.

Psalm 41:1

But whoso hath this world's good, and seeth his brother have need, and shutteth up his bowels of compassion from him, how dwelleth the love of God in him?

My little children, let us not love in word, neither in tongue; but in deed and in truth.

1 John 3:17,18

He answereth and saith unto them, He that hath two coats, let him impart to him that hath none; and he that hath meat, let him do likewise.

Luke 3:11

He that despiseth his neighbour sinneth: but he that hath mercy on the poor, happy is he.

He that oppresseth the poor reproacheth his Maker: but he that honoureth him hath mercy on the poor.   *Proverbs 14:21,31*

He that oppresseth the poor to increase his riches, and he that giveth to the rich, shall surely come to want.

Rob not the poor, because he is poor: neither oppress the afflicted in the gate.

Proverbs 22:16,22

Defend the poor and fatherless: do justice to the afflicted and needy.   *Psalm 82:3*

He that hath pity upon the poor lendeth unto the Lord; and that which he hath given will he pay him again.   *Proverbs 19:17*

He that giveth unto the poor shall not lack: but he that hideth his eyes shall have many a curse.

Proverbs 28:27

Jesus said unto him, If thou wilt be perfect, go and sell that thou hast, and give to the poor, and thou shalt have treasure in heaven: and come and follow me.   *Matthew 19:21*

GOD'S COVENANT WORD ON:

ESTABLISHING A HOME

Through wisdom is an house builded; and by understanding it is established:

And by knowledge shall the chambers be filled with all precious and pleasant riches.

Proverbs 24:3,4

Therefore whosoever heareth these sayings of mine, and doeth them, I will liken him unto a wise man, which built his house upon a rock: And the rain descended, and the floods came, and the winds blew, and beat upon that house; and it fell not; for it was founded upon a rock.

Matthew 7:24,25

For other foundation can no man lay than that is laid, which is Jesus Christ. *1 Corinthians 3:11*

Now therefore ye are no more strangers and foreigners, but fellowcitizens with the saints, and of the household of God;

And are built upon the foundation of the apostles and prophets, Jesus Christ himself being the chief corner stone;

In whom all the building fitly framed together groweth unto an holy temple in the Lord:

In whom ye also are builded together for an habitation of God through the Spirit.

Ephesians 2:19-22

Every wise woman buildeth her house: but the foolish plucketh it down with her hands.

Proverbs 14:1

House and riches are the inheritance of fathers: and a prudent wife is from the Lord.

Proverbs 19:14

I will behave myself wisely in a perfect way. O when wilt thou come unto me? I will walk within my house with a perfect heart.   *Psalm 101:2*

Peace be within thy walls, and prosperity within thy palaces. *Psalm 122:7*

GOD'S COVENANT WORD ON:

PROTECTION OF THE HOME

And my people shall dwell in a peaceable habitation, and in sure dwellings, and in quiet resting places. *Isaiah 32:18*

And of Benjamin he [Moses] said, The beloved of the Lord shall dwell in safety by him; and the Lord shall cover him all the day long, and he shall dwell between his shoulders.

Deuteronomy 33:12

The name of the Lord is a strong tower: the righteous runneth into it, and is safe.

Proverbs 18:10

Lay not wait, O wicked man, against the dwelling of the righteous; spoil not his resting place.

Proverbs 24:15

And every one that hath forsaken houses, or brethren, or sisters, or father, or mother, or wife, or children, or lands, for my name's sake, shall receive an hundredfold, and shall inherit everlasting life.

Matthew 19:29

Because thou hast made the Lord, which is my refuge, even the most High, thy habitation;

There shall no evil befall thee, neither shall any plague come nigh thy dwelling.

For he shall give his angels charge over thee, to keep thee in all thy ways.   *Psalm 91:9-11*

The angel of the Lord encampeth round about them that fear him, and delivereth them.

Psalm 34:7

In the house of the righteous is much treasure: but in the revenues of the wicked is trouble.

Proverbs 15:6

He [the Lord] blesseth the habitation of the just.

Proverbs 3:33

The house of the righteous shall stand.

Proverbs 12:7

GOD'S
COVENANT
BLESSINGS
FOR YOU

PART 6

GOD'S
COVENANT
BLESSINGS FOR
MY HEALTH

Covenant Truth About:

Fasting

Daniel purposed in his heart that he would not defile himself with the portion of the king's meat, nor with the wine which he drank: therefore he requested of the prince of the eunuchs that he might not defile himself.... Prove thy servants, I beseech thee, ten days; and let them give us pulse to eat, and water to drink.... So he consented to them in this matter, and proved them ten days. And at the end of ten days their countenances appeared fairer and fatter in flesh than all the children which did eat the portion of the king's meat.

Daniel 1:8,12,14,15

Neither have I gone back from the commandment of his lips; I have esteemed the words of his mouth more than my necessary food. *Job 23:12*

Moreover when ye fast, be not, as the hypocrites, of a sad countenance: for they disfigure their faces, that they may appear unto men to fast. Verily I say unto you, They have their reward. But thou, when thou fastest, anoint thine head, and wash thy face; That thou appear not unto men to fast, but unto thy Father which is in secret: and thy Father, which seeth in secret, shall reward thee openly.

Matthew 6:16-18

Is not this the fast that I have chosen? to loose the bands of wickedness, to undo the heavy burdens, and to let the oppressed go free, and that ye break every yoke?

Isaiah 58:6

Sanctify ye a fast, call a solemn assembly, gather the elders and all the inhabitants of the land into the house of the Lord your God, and cry unto the Lord.

Joel 1:14

Covenant Truth About:

Healthy Eating

Feed me with food convenient for me.

Proverbs 30:8

Who satisfieth thy mouth with good things; so that thy youth is renewed like the eagle's.

Psalm 103:5

But I keep under my body, and bring it into subjection: lest that by any means, when I have preached to others, I myself should be a castaway.

1 Corinthians 9:27

All things are lawful unto me, but all things are not expedient: all things are lawful for me, but I will not be brought under the power of any.

1 Corinthians 6:12

Now therefore beware, I pray thee, and drink not wine nor strong drink, and eat not any unclean thing. *Judges 13:4*

Be not among winebibbers; among riotous eaters of flesh:
For the drunkard and the glutton shall come to poverty: and drowsiness shall clothe a man with rags. *Proverbs 23:20,21*

There hath no temptation taken you but such as is common to man: but God is faithful, who will not suffer you to be tempted above that ye are able; but will with the temptation also make a way to escape, that ye may be able to bear it.
1 Corinthians 10:13

Whether therefore ye eat, or drink, or whatsoever ye do, do all to the glory of God.
1 Corinthians 10:31

COVENANT TRUTH ABOUT:

PHYSICAL EXERCISE

What? know ye not that your body is the temple of the Holy Ghost which is in you, which ye have of God, and ye are not your own?

For ye are bought with a price: therefore glorify God in your body, and in your spirit, which are God's. *1 Corinthians 6:19,20*

Know ye not that they which run in a race run all, but one receiveth the prize? So run, that ye may obtain.

And every man that striveth for the mastery is temperate in all things. Now they do it to obtain a corruptible crown; but we an incorruptible.

I therefore so run, not as uncertainly; so fight I, not as one that beateth the air:

But I keep under my body, and bring it into subjection: lest that by any means, when I have

preached to others, I myself should be a castaway.
1 Corinthians 9:24-27

I can do all things through Christ which strengtheneth me.   *Philippians 4:13*

For by thee I have run through a troop: by my God have I leaped over a wall.... God is my strength and power: and he maketh my way perfect.
2 Samuel 22:30,33

The glory of young men is their strength.
Proverbs 20:29

Who can find a virtuous woman? for her price is far above rubies. She girdeth her loins with strength, and strengtheneth her arms.
Proverbs 31:10,17

But they that wait upon the Lord shall renew their strength; they shall mount up with wings as eagles; they shall run, and not be weary; and they shall walk, and not faint.   *Isaiah 40:31*

Covenant Truth About:

Alcoholism

And be not drunk with wine, wherein is excess; but be filled with the Spirit.   *Ephesians 5:18*

It is not for kings, O Lemuel, it is not for kings to drink wine; nor for princes strong drink: Lest they drink, and forget the law, and pervert the judgment of any of the afflicted. *Proverbs 31:4,5*

Woe unto them that rise up early in the morning, that they may follow strong drink; that continue until night, till wine inflame them!

Isaiah 5:11

Be not among winebibbers; among riotous eaters of flesh:

For the drunkard and the glutton shall come to poverty: and drowsiness shall clothe a man with rags.

Who hath woe? who hath sorrow? who hath contentions? who hath babbling? who hath wounds without cause? who hath redness of eyes?

They that tarry long at the wine; they that go to seek mixed wine.

Look not thou upon the wine when it is red, when it giveth his colour in the cup, when it moveth itself aright.

At the last it biteth like a serpent, and stingeth like an adder.

Thine eyes shall behold strange women, and thine heart shall utter perverse things.

Proverbs 23:20,21,29-33

It is good neither to eat flesh, nor to drink wine, nor any thing whereby thy brother stumbleth, or is offended, or is made weak.

Romans 14:21

Forgetting those things which are behind, and reaching forth unto those things which are before,

I press toward the mark for the prize of the high calling of God in Christ Jesus.

Philippians 3:13,14

And every man that striveth for the mastery is temperate in all things.   *1 Corinthians 9:25*

Covenant Truth About:

Smoking

There is a way which seemeth right unto a man, but the end thereof are the ways of death.

Proverbs 14:12

What? know ye not that your body is the temple of the Holy Ghost which is in you, which ye have of God, and ye are not your own?

For ye are bought with a price: therefore glorify God in your body, and in your spirit, which are God's. *1 Corinthians 6:19,20*

If any man defile the temple of God, him shall God destroy; for the temple of God is holy, which temple ye are. *1 Corinthians 3:17*

Let not sin therefore reign in your mortal body, that ye should obey it in the lusts thereof.

Romans 6:12

I beseech you therefore, brethren, by the mercies of God, that ye present your bodies a living sacrifice, holy, acceptable unto God, which is your reasonable service.

And be not conformed to this world: but be ye transformed by the renewing of your mind, that ye may prove what is that good, and acceptable, and perfect, will of God.   *Romans 12:1,2*

And they that are Christ's have crucified the flesh with the affections and lusts. If we live in the Spirit, let us also walk in the Spirit.

Galatians 5:24,25

Ye are of God, little children, and have overcome them: because greater is he that is in you, than he that is in the world.   *1 John 4:4*

Having therefore these promises, dearly beloved, let us cleanse ourselves from all filthiness of the flesh and spirit, perfecting holiness in the fear of God.   *2 Corinthians 7:1*

COVENANT TRUTH ABOUT:

PHYSICAL HEALING

Beloved, I wish above all things that thou mayest prosper and be in health, even as thy soul prospereth. *3 John 2*

I will put none of these diseases upon thee, which I have brought upon the Egyptians: for I am the Lord that healeth thee. *Exodus 15:26*

But he was wounded for our transgressions, he was bruised for our iniquities: the chastisement of our peace was upon him; and with his stripes we are healed. *Isaiah 53:5*

How God anointed Jesus of Nazareth with the Holy Ghost and with power: who went about doing good, and healing all that were oppressed of the devil; for God was with him. *Acts 10:38*

I will take sickness away from the midst of thee.

Exodus 23:25

Bless the Lord, O my soul, and forget not all his benefits:

Who forgiveth all thine iniquities; who healeth all thy diseases.

Psalm 103:2,3

My son, attend to my words.... For they are life unto those that find them, and health to all their flesh.

Proverbs 4:20,22

He sent his word, and healed them, and delivered them from their destructions.

Psalm 107:20

Speak the word only, and my servant shall be healed.

Matthew 8:8

He [Jesus] cast out the spirits with his word, and healed all that were sick: That it might be fulfilled which was spoken by Esaias the prophet, saying, Himself took our infirmities, and bare our sicknesses. *Matthew 8:16,17*

They [believers] shall lay hands on the sick, and they shall recover. *Mark 16:18*

COVENANT TRUTH ABOUT:

MENTAL HEALING

Thou wilt keep him in perfect peace, whose mind is stayed on thee.   *Isaiah 26:3*

God is not the author of confusion, but of peace.
                                    1 Corinthians 14:33

Be not conformed to this world: but be ye transformed by the renewing of your mind.
                                    Romans 12:2

Let this mind be in you, which was also in Christ Jesus.   *Philippians 2:5*

For who hath known the mind of the Lord, that he may instruct him? But we have the mind of Christ.   *1 Corinthians 2:16*

Finally, brethren, whatsoever things are true, whatsoever things are honest, whatsoever things are just, whatsoever things are pure, whatsoever things are lovely, whatsoever thing are of good report; if there be any virtue, and if there be any praise, think on these things.   *Philippians 4:8*

Fear thou not; for I am with thee: be not dismayed; for I am thy God: I will strengthen thee; yea, I will help thee; yea, I will uphold thee with the right hand of my righteousness.

Isaiah 41:10

For God hath not given us the spirit of fear; but of power, and of love, and of a sound mind.

2 Timothy 1:7

For the Lord God will help me; therefore shall I not be confounded: therefore have I set my face like a flint, and I know that I shall not be ashamed.

Isaiah 50:7

And the peace of God, which passeth all understanding, shall keep your hearts and minds through Christ Jesus. *Philippians 4:7*

COVENANT TRUTH ABOUT:

EMOTIONAL HEALING

Come unto me, all ye that labour and are heavy laden, and I will give you rest. Take my yoke upon you, and learn of me; for I am meek and lowly in heart: and ye shall find rest unto your souls.   *Matthew 11:28,29*

Follow peace with all men, and holiness, without which no man shall see the Lord:
Looking diligently lest any man fail of the grace of God; lest any root of bitterness springing up trouble you, and thereby many be defiled.

Hebrews 12:14,15

Let all bitterness, and wrath, and anger, and clamour, and evil speaking, be put away from you, with all malice:
And be ye kind one to another, tenderhearted, forgiving one another, even as God for Christ's sake hath forgiven you.   *Ephesians 4:31,32*

The Lord also will be a refuge for the oppressed, a refuge in times of trouble. *Psalm 9:9*

He healeth the broken in heart, and bindeth up their wounds. *Psalm 147:3*

They that sow in tears shall reap in joy.
Psalm 126:5

Peace I leave with you, my peace I give unto you: not as the world giveth, give I unto you. Let not your heart be troubled, neither let it be afraid.
John 14:27

In God have I put my trust: I will not be afraid what man can do unto me. *Psalm 56:11*

The Spirit of the Lord is upon me, because he hath anointed me to preach the gospel to the poor; he hath sent me to heal the brokenhearted, to preach deliverance to the captives, and recovering of sight to the blind, to set at liberty them that are bruised. *Luke 4:18*

GOD'S
COVENANT
BLESSINGS
FOR YOU

PART 7

GOD'S
COVENANT
BLESSINGS FOR
WHEN I FEEL:

God's Covenant Blessings
For When I Feel:

Abused

When my father and my mother forsake me, then the Lord will take me up.   *Psalm 27:10*

Look upon mine affliction and my pain; and forgive all my sins.

Consider mine enemies; for they are many; and they hate me with cruel hatred.

O keep my soul, and deliver me: let me not be ashamed; for I put my trust in thee.

Psalm 25:18-20

Take heed to yourselves: If thy brother trespass against thee, rebuke him; and if he repent, forgive him.   *Luke 17:3*

Forgive, I pray thee now, the trespass of thy brethren, and their sin; for they did unto thee evil:.... And Joseph said unto them, Fear not: for am I in the place of God? But as for you, ye thought evil against me; but God meant it unto good.

Genesis 50:17,19,20

Then came Peter to him [Jesus], and said, Lord, how oft shall my brother sin against me, and I forgive him? till seven times? Jesus saith unto him, I say not unto thee, Until seven times: but, Until seventy times seven. *Matthew 18:21,22*

Judge not, and ye shall not be judged: condemn not, and ye shall not be condemned: forgive, and ye shall be forgiven. *Luke 6:37*

For if ye forgive men their trespasses, your heavenly Father will also forgive you.

Matthew 6:14

And God shall wipe away all tears from their eyes; and there shall be no more death, neither sorrow, nor crying, neither shall there be any more pain: for the former things are passed away. *Revelation 21:4*

God's Covenant Blessings
For When I Feel:

Anxious

Peace I leave with you, my peace I give unto you: not as the world giveth, give I unto you. Let not your heart be troubled, neither let it be afraid.
John 14:27

Be careful for nothing; but in every thing by prayer and supplication with thanksgiving let your requests be made known unto God.

And the peace of God, which passeth all understanding, shall keep your hearts and minds through Christ Jesus. *Philippians 4:6,7*

Therefore I say unto you, Take no thought for your life, what ye shall eat, or what ye shall drink; nor yet for your body, what ye shall put on. Is not the life more than meat, and the body than raiment? Behold the fowls of the air: for they sow not, neither do they reap, nor gather into barns; yet your heavenly Father feedeth them. Are ye not much better than they? Which of you by taking thought can add one cubit unto his stature? And why take ye thought for raiment? Consider the lilies of the field, how they grow; they toil not, neither do they spin: And yet I say unto you, That even Solomon in all his glory was not arrayed like one of these. Wherefore, if God so clothe the grass of the field, which to day is, and to morrow is cast into the oven, shall he not much more clothe you, O ye of little faith? Therefore take no thought, saying, What shall we eat? or, What shall we drink? or, Wherewithal shall we be clothed? (For after all these things do the Gentiles seek:) for your heavenly Father knoweth that ye have need of all these things. But seek ye first the kingdom of God, and his righteousness; and all these things shall be added unto you. *Matthew 6:25-33*

GOD'S COVENANT BLESSINGS
FOR WHEN I FEEL:

BITTER

Follow peace with all men, and holiness, without which no man shall see the Lord:

Looking diligently lest any man fail of the grace of God; lest any root of bitterness springing up trouble you, and thereby many be defiled.

Hebrews 12:14,15

But if ye have bitter envying and strife in your hearts, glory not, and lie not against the truth.

This wisdom descendeth not from above, but is earthly, sensual, devilish.

For where envying and strife is, there is confusion and every evil work.   *James 3:14-16*

Thou [Simon the sorcerer] hast neither part nor lot in this matter: for thy heart is not right in the sight of God. Repent therefore of this thy wickedness, and pray God, if perhaps the thought of thine heart may be forgiven thee. For I [Peter] perceive that thou art in the gall of bitterness, and in the bond of iniquity.   *Acts 8:21-23*

Let all bitterness, and wrath, and anger, and clamour, and evil speaking, be put away from you, with all malice:

And be ye kind one to another, tenderhearted, forgiving one another, even as God for Christ's sake hath forgiven you.   *Ephesians 4:31,32*

When he [Jesus] was reviled, [he] reviled not again; when he suffered, he threatened not; but committed himself to him that judgeth righteously.   *1 Peter 2:23*

Then said Jesus, Father, forgive them; for they know not what they do. And they parted his raiment, and cast lots.   *Luke 23:34*

GOD'S COVENANT BLESSINGS
FOR WHEN I FEEL:

CONTROLLED

The Spirit of the Lord God is upon me; because the Lord hath anointed me to preach good tidings unto the meek; he hath sent me to bind up the brokenhearted, to proclaim liberty to the captives, and the opening of the prison to them that are bound.   *Isaiah 61:1*

And ye shall know the truth, and the truth shall make you free.... If the Son therefore shall make you free, ye shall be free indeed.   *John 8:32,36*

Is not this the fast that I have chosen? to loose the bands of wickedness, to undo the heavy burdens, and to let the oppressed go free, and that ye break every yoke?   *Isaiah 58:6*

God setteth the solitary in families: he bringeth out those which are bound with chains.

Psalm 68:6

Then saith Jesus unto him, Get thee hence, Satan: for it is written, Thou shalt worship the Lord thy God, and him only shalt thou serve. Then the devil leaveth him, and, behold, angels came and ministered unto him. *Matthew 4:10,11*

Stand fast therefore in the liberty wherewith Christ hath made us free, and be not entangled again with the yoke of bondage. *Galatians 5:1*

And I will give unto thee the keys of the kingdom of heaven: and whatsoever thou shalt bind on earth shall be bound in heaven: and whatsoever thou shalt loose on earth shall be loosed in heaven. *Matthew 16:19*

For though I be free from all men, yet have I made myself servant unto all, that I might gain the more. *1 Corinthians 9:19*

GOD'S COVENANT BLESSINGS
FOR WHEN I FEEL:

CRITICAL

Blessed is the man that walketh not in the counsel of the ungodly, nor standeth in the way of sinners, nor sitteth in the seat of the scornful.

Psalm 1:1

Now I beseech you, brethren, by the name of our Lord Jesus Christ, that ye all speak the same thing, and that there be no divisions among you; but that ye be perfectly joined together in the same mind and in the same judgment.

1 Corinthians 1:10

Let us not therefore judge one another any more: but judge this rather, that no man put a stumblingblock or an occasion to fall in his brother's way.

Romans 14:13

Therefore thou art inexcusable, O man, whosoever thou art that judgest: for wherein thou judgest another, thou condemnest thyself; for thou that judgest doest the same things.

Romans 2:1

So when they [the Scribes and Pharisees] continued asking him [Jesus], he lifted up himself, and said unto them, He that is without sin among you, let him first cast a stone at her.

John 8:7

Speak not evil one of another, brethren.

James 4:11

Judge not, that ye be not judged. For with what judgment ye judge, ye shall be judged: and with what measure ye mete, it shall be measured to you again. And why beholdest thou the mote that is in thy brother's eye, but considerest not the beam that is in thine own eye? *Matthew 7:1-3*

Keep thy tongue from evil, and thy lips from speaking guile.   *Psalm 34:13*

GOD'S COVENANT BLESSINGS
FOR WHEN I FEEL:

CRITICIZED

Reproach hath broken my heart; and I am full of heaviness: and I looked for some to take pity, but there was none; and for comforters, but I found none.

But I am poor and sorrowful: let thy salvation, O God, set me up on high. *Psalm 69:20,29*

Plead my cause, O Lord, with them that strive with me: fight against them that fight against me.
Psalm 35:1

Blessed are ye, when men shall revile you, and persecute you, and shall say all manner of evil against you falsely, for my sake. *Matthew 5:11*

If ye be reproached for the name of Christ, happy are ye; for the spirit of glory and of God resteth upon you: on their part he is evil spoken of, but on your part he is glorified.   *1 Peter 4:14*

When he [Jesus] was reviled, [he] reviled not again; when he suffered, he threatened not; but committed himself to him that judgeth righteously.
1 Peter 2:23

No weapon that is formed against thee shall prosper; and every tongue that shall rise against thee in judgment thou shalt condemn. This is the heritage of the servants of the Lord, and their righteousness is of me, saith the Lord.
Isaiah 54:17

Blessed are ye, when men shall hate you, and when they shall separate you from their company, and shall reproach you, and cast out your name as evil, for the Son of man's sake. Rejoice ye in that day, and leap for joy: for, behold, your reward is great in heaven: for in the like manner did their fathers unto the prophets.   *Luke 6:22,23*

GOD'S COVENANT BLESSINGS
FOR WHEN I FEEL:

FRUSTRATED

When the waves of death compassed me, the floods of ungodly men made me afraid; The sorrows of hell compassed me about; the snares of death prevented me; In my distress I called upon the Lord, and cried to my God: and he did hear my voice out of his temple, and my cry did enter into his ears. Then the earth shook and trembled; the foundations of heaven moved and shook, because he was wroth.... The Lord thundered from heaven, and the most High uttered his voice.... He delivered me from my strong enemy, and from them that hated me: for they were too strong for me.... He brought me forth also into a large place: he delivered me, because he delighted in me.

2 Samuel 22:5-8,14,18,20

Let us not be weary in well doing: for in due season we shall reap, if we faint not.

Galatians 6:9

Ye have need of patience, that, after ye have done the will of God, ye might receive the promise.

Hebrews 10:36

Thou wilt keep him in perfect peace, whose mind is stayed on thee: because he trusteth in thee. Trust ye in the Lord for ever: for in the Lord Jehovah is everlasting strength.

Isaiah 26:3,4

But if we hope for that we see not, then do we with patience wait for it. *Romans 8:25*

And we desire that every one of you do shew the same diligence to the full assurance of hope unto the end. *Hebrews 6:11*

Behold, we count them happy which endure.

James 5:11

GOD'S COVENANT BLESSINGS
FOR WHEN I FEEL:

HOPELESS

Why art thou cast down, O my soul? and why art thou disquieted in me? hope thou in God: for I shall yet praise him for the help of his countenance. *Psalm 42:5*

Hope deferred maketh the heart sick: but when the desire cometh, it is a tree of life.

Proverbs 13:12

Therefore my heart is glad, and my glory rejoiceth: my flesh also shall rest in hope.

Psalm 16:9

The Lord is my rock, and my fortress, and my deliverer; my God, my strength, in whom I will trust; my buckler, and the horn of my salvation, and my high tower. *Psalm 18:2*

The Lord is my portion, saith my soul; therefore will I hope in him.... It is good that a man should both hope and quietly wait for the salvation of the Lord.   *Lamentations 3:24,26*

And we desire that every one of you do shew the same diligence to the full assurance of hope unto the end:

Which hope we have as an anchor of the soul, both sure and stedfast, and which entereth into that within the veil.   *Hebrews 6:11,19*

And hope maketh not ashamed; because the love of God is shed abroad in our hearts by the Holy Ghost which is given unto us.   *Romans 5:5*

Be of good courage, and he shall strengthen your heart, all ye that hope in the Lord.   *Psalm 31:24*

Now the God of hope fill you with all joy and peace in believing, that ye may abound in hope, through the power of the Holy Ghost.

Romans 15:13

GOD'S COVENANT BLESSINGS
FOR WHEN I FEEL:

JEALOUS

But if ye have bitter envying and strife in your hearts, glory not, and lie not against the truth.

This wisdom descendeth not from above, but is earthly, sensual, devilish.

For where envying and strife is, there is confusion and every evil work.   *James 3:14-16*

Set me as a seal upon thine heart, as a seal upon thine arm: for love is strong as death; jealousy is cruel as the grave: the coals thereof are coals of fire, which hath a most vehement flame.

Song of Solomon 8:6

For jealousy is the rage of a man: therefore he will not spare in the day of vengeance.

Proverbs 6:34

Wrath is cruel, and anger is outrageous; but who is able to stand before envy?   *Proverbs 27:4*

A sound heart is the life of the flesh: but envy the rottenness of the bones.   *Proverbs 14:30*

Let not thine heart envy sinners: but be thou in the fear of the Lord all the day long.
Proverbs 23:17

Let your conversation be without covetousness; and be content with such things as ye have: for he hath said, I will never leave thee, nor forsake thee.   *Hebrews 13:5*

But godliness with contentment is great gain.
For we brought nothing into this world, and it is certain we can carry nothing out.
And having food and raiment let us be therewith content.   *1 Timothy 6:6-8*

Not that I speak in respect of want: for I have learned, in whatsoever state I am, therewith to be content. *Philippians 4:11*

GOD'S COVENANT BLESSINGS
FOR WHEN I FEEL:

SELF-PITY

I am crucified with Christ: nevertheless I live; yet not I, but Christ liveth in me: and the life which I now live in the flesh I live by the faith of the Son of God, who loved me, and gave himself for me.

Galatians 2:20

Let this mind be in you, which was also in Christ Jesus:

Who, being in the form of God, thought it not robbery to be equal with God:

But made himself of no reputation, and took upon him the form of a servant, and was made in the likeness of men:

And being found in fashion as a man, he humbled himself, and became obedient unto death, even the death of the cross.

Philippians 2:5-8

Fret not thyself because of evildoers, neither be thou envious against the workers of iniquity.

Delight thyself also in the Lord; and he shall give thee the desires of thine heart.

Commit thy way unto the Lord; trust also in him; and he shall bring it to pass.

And he shall bring forth thy righteousness as the light, and thy judgment as the noonday.

Rest in the Lord, and wait patiently for him: fret not thyself because of him who prospereth in his way, because of the man who bringeth wicked devices to pass. Cease from anger, and forsake wrath: fret not thyself in any wise to do evil.

Psalm 37:1,4-8

Finally, brethren, whatsoever things are true, whatsoever things are honest, whatsoever things are just, whatsoever things are pure, whatsoever things are lovely, whatsoever thing are of good report; if there be any virtue, and if there be any praise, think on these things. *Philippians 4:8*

GOD'S
COVENANT
BLESSINGS
FOR YOU

PART 8

COVENANT
BLESSINGS FOR
WHEN I'M:

COVENANT BLESSINGS
FOR WHEN I'M:

STRUGGLING WITH GUILT

Come now, and let us reason together, saith the Lord: though your sins be as scarlet, they shall be as white as snow; though they be red like crimson, they shall be as wool.   *Isaiah 1:18*

Thou, Lord, art good, and ready to forgive; and plenteous in mercy unto all them that call upon thee.   *Psalm 86:5*

He that covereth his sins shall not prosper: but whoso confesseth and forsaketh them shall have mercy.   *Proverbs 28:13*

If we confess our sins, he is faithful and just to forgive us our sins, and to cleanse us from all unrighteousness.   *1 John 1:9*

Their sins and their iniquities will I remember no more.   *Hebrews 8:12*

There is therefore now no condemnation to them which are in Christ Jesus, who walk not after the flesh, but after the Spirit.   *Romans 8:1*

In whom [Jesus] we have redemption through his blood, the forgiveness of sins, according to the riches of his grace.   *Ephesians 1:7*

I, even I, am he that blotteth out thy transgressions for mine own sake, and will not remember thy sins.   *Isaiah 43:25*

Blessed are they whose iniquities are forgiven, and whose sins are covered.   *Romans 4:7*

Forgetting those things which are behind, and reaching forth unto those things which are before,
I press toward the mark for the prize of the high calling of God in Christ Jesus.
Philippians 3:13,14

COVENANT BLESSINGS
FOR WHEN I'M:

TEMPTED TO HATE

Thou shalt not hate thy brother in thine heart.
Leviticus 19:17

Whosoever hateth his brother is a murderer: and ye know that no murderer hath eternal life abiding in him. *1 John 3:15*

He that saith he is in the light, and hateth his brother, is in darkness even until now.
But he that hateth his brother is in darkness, and walketh in darkness, and knoweth not whither he goeth, because that darkness hath blinded his eyes. *1 John 2:9,11*

If a man say, I love God, and hateth his brother, he is a liar: for he that loveth not his brother whom he hath seen, how can he love God whom he hath not seen? *1 John 4:20*

We ourselves also were sometimes foolish, disobedient, deceived, serving divers lusts and pleasures, living in malice and envy, hateful, and hating one another.

But after that the kindness and love of God our Saviour toward man appeared...according to his mercy he saved us....   *Titus 3:3-5*

Wherefore laying aside all malice, and all guile, and hypocrisies, and envies, and all evil speakings,

As newborn babes, desire the sincere milk of the word, that ye may grow thereby.   *1 Peter 2:1,2*

Let all bitterness, and wrath, and anger, and clamour, and evil speaking, be put away from you, with all malice.   *Ephesians 4:31*

Ye have heard that it hath been said, Thou shalt love thy neighbour, and hate thine enemy. But I say unto you, Love your enemies, bless them that curse you, do good to them that hate you, and pray for them which despitefully use you, and persecute you.   *Matthew 5:43,44*

COVENANT BLESSINGS
FOR WHEN I'M:

LACKING DIRECTION

Elijah came unto all the people, and said, How long halt ye between two opinions? if the Lord be God, follow him. *1 Kings 18:21*

No man can serve two masters: for either he will hate the one, and love the other; or else he will hold to the one, and despise the other. Ye cannot serve God and mammon. *Matthew 6:24*

Draw nigh to God, and he will draw nigh to you. Cleanse your hands, ye sinners; and purify your hearts, ye double minded. *James 4:8*

A double minded man is unstable in all his ways. *James 1:8*

Teach me thy way, O Lord, and lead me in a plain path, because of mine enemies.

Psalm 27:11

Thy word is a lamp unto my feet, and a light unto my path. *Psalm 119:105*

Ponder the path of thy feet, and let all thy ways be established. *Proverbs 4:26*

The path of the just is as the shining light, that shineth more and more unto the perfect day.

Proverbs 4:18

A man's heart deviseth his way: but the Lord directeth his steps. *Proverbs 16:9*

Trust in the Lord with all thine heart; and lean not unto thine own understanding. In all thy ways acknowledge him, and he shall direct thy paths.

Proverbs 3:5,6

Therefore, my beloved brethren, be ye stedfast, unmoveable, always abounding in the work of the Lord, forasmuch as ye know that your labour is not in vain in the Lord.   *1 Corinthians 15:58*

COVENANT BLESSINGS
FOR WHEN I'M:

INDIFFERENT

Afterward he [Jesus] appeared unto the eleven as they sat at meat, and upbraided them with their unbelief and hardness of heart, because they believed not them which had seen him after he was risen. *Mark 16:14*

So then because thou art lukewarm, and neither cold nor hot, I will spue thee out of my mouth.

Because thou sayest, I am rich, and increased with goods, and have need of nothing; and knowest not that thou art wretched, and miserable, and poor, and blind, and naked:

As many as I love, I rebuke and chasten: be zealous therefore, and repent.

Behold, I stand at the door, and knock: if any man hear my voice, and open the door, I will come in to him, and will sup with him, and he with me.

Revelation 3:16,17,19,20

A new heart also will I give you, and a new spirit will I put within you: and I will take away the stony heart out of your flesh, and I will give you an heart of flesh. And I will put my spirit within you, and cause you to walk in my statutes, and ye shall keep my judgments, and do them.   *Ezekiel 36:26,27*

Let your heart therefore be perfect with the Lord our God, to walk in his statutes, and to keep his commandments, as at this day.   *1 Kings 8:61*

Brethren, I count not myself to have apprehended: but this one thing I do, forgetting those things which are behind, and reaching forth unto those things which are before,

I press toward the mark....

Let us therefore, as many as be perfect, be thus minded: and if in any thing ye be otherwise minded, God shall reveal even this unto you.

Philippians 3:13-15

COVENANT BLESSINGS
FOR WHEN I'M:

INSECURE

He that dwelleth in the secret place of the most High shall abide under the shadow of the Almighty.

He shall cover thee with his feathers, and under his wings shalt thou trust: his truth shall be thy shield and buckler. *Psalm 91:1,4*

The angel of the Lord encampeth round about them that fear him, and delivereth them.

Psalm 34:7

I can do all things through Christ which strengtheneth me. *Philippians 4:13*

Being confident of this very thing, that he which hath begun a good work in you will perform it until the day of Jesus Christ. *Philippians 1:6*

What shall we then say to these things? If God be for us, who can be against us? He that spared not his own Son, but delivered him up for us all, how shall he not with him also freely give us all things? *Romans 8:31,32*

Have not I commanded thee? Be strong and of a good courage; be not afraid, neither be thou dismayed: for the Lord thy God is with thee whithersoever thou goest. *Joshua 1:9*

Fear thou not; for I am with thee: be not dismayed; for I am thy God: I will strengthen thee; yea, I will help thee; yea, I will uphold thee with the right hand of my righteousness.... For I the Lord thy God will hold thy right hand, saying unto thee, Fear not; I will help thee.

Isaiah 41:10,13

So that we may boldly say, The Lord is my helper, and I will not fear what man shall do unto me.

Hebrews 13:6

COVENANT BLESSINGS
FOR WHEN I'M:

NERVOUS

He shall not be afraid of evil tidings: his heart is fixed, trusting in the Lord.   *Psalm 112:7*

I was dumb with silence, I held my peace, even from good; and my sorrow was stirred.

My heart was hot within me, while I was musing the fire burned: then spake I with my tongue,

Lord, make me to know mine end, and the measure of my days, what it is: that I may know how frail I am.   *Psalm 39:2-4*

But he was wounded for our transgressions, he was bruised for our iniquities: the chastisement of our peace was upon him; and with his stripes we are healed.   *Isaiah 53:5*

The Lord will give strength unto his people; the Lord will bless his people with peace.

Psalm 29:11

The God of all grace, who hath called us unto his eternal glory by Christ Jesus, after that ye have suffered a while, make you perfect, stablish, strengthen, settle you.　　*1 Peter 5:10*

...I bow my knees unto the Father of our Lord Jesus Christ,

That he would grant you, according to the riches of his glory, to be strengthened with might by his Spirit in the inner man.

Ephesians 3:14,16

The Lord is faithful, who shall stablish you, and keep you from evil.　　*2 Thessalonians 3:3*

The work of righteousness shall be peace; and the effect of righteousness quietness and assurance for ever.　　*Isaiah 32:17*

I will both lay me down in peace, and sleep: for thou, Lord, only makest me dwell in safety.

Psalm 4:8

My heart is fixed, O God, my heart is fixed: I will sing and give praise. *Psalm 57:7*

COVENANT BLESSINGS
FOR WHEN I'M:

BATTLING PRIDE

A man's pride shall bring him low: but honour shall uphold the humble in spirit.

Proverbs 29:23

When pride cometh, then cometh shame: but with the lowly is wisdom. *Proverbs 11:2*

The fear of the Lord is to hate evil: pride, and arrogancy, and the evil way, and the froward mouth, do I hate. *Proverbs 8:13*

Thou shalt remember all the way which the Lord thy God led thee these forty years in the wilderness, to humble thee, and to prove thee, to know what was in thine heart, whether thou wouldest keep his commandments, or no.

Deuteronomy 8:2

He forgetteth not the cry of the humble.

Psalm 9:12

If my people, which are called by my name, shall humble themselves, and pray, and seek my face, and turn from their wicked ways; then will I hear from heaven, and will forgive their sin, and will heal their land.   *2 Chronicles 7:14*

Whosoever therefore shall humble himself as this little child, the same is greatest in the kingdom of heaven.   *Matthew 18:4*

And whosoever shall exalt himself shall be abased; and he that shall humble himself shall be exalted.   *Matthew 23:12*

But he giveth more grace. Wherefore he saith, God resisteth the proud, but giveth grace unto the humble.   *James 4:6*

Humble yourselves therefore under the mighty hand of God, that he may exalt you in due time.   *1 Peter 5:6*

COVENANT BLESSINGS
FOR WHEN I'M:

SENSING REJECTION

When my father and my mother forsake me, then the Lord will take me up.   *Psalm 27:10*

Can a woman forget her sucking child, that she should not have compassion on the son of her womb? yea, they may forget, yet will I not forget thee.   *Isaiah 49:15*

The Lord will not forsake his people for his great name's sake: because it hath pleased the Lord to make you his people.   *1 Samuel 12:22*

The Lord will not cast off his people, neither will he forsake his inheritance.   *Psalm 94:14*

What glory is it, if, when ye be buffeted for your faults, ye shall take it patiently? but if, when ye do well, and suffer for it, ye take it patiently, this is acceptable with God.   *1 Peter 2:20*

He [Jesus] said, Verily I say unto you, No prophet is accepted in his own country.

Luke 4:24

Be strong and of a good courage, fear not, nor be afraid of them: for the Lord thy God, he´ it is that doth go with thee; he will not fail thee, nor forsake thee.   *Deuteronomy 31:6*

Whereas thou hast been forsaken and hated, so that no man went through thee, I will make thee an eternal excellency, a joy of many generations.

Isaiah 60:15

Thou shalt no more be termed Forsaken; neither shall thy land any more be termed Desolate.

Isaiah 62:4

(The Lord thy God is a merciful God;) he will not forsake thee.   *Deuteronomy 4:31*

To the praise of the glory of his grace, wherein he hath made us accepted in the beloved.

Ephesians 1:6

Covenant Blessings
For When I'm:

Resentful

But love ye your enemies, and do good, and lend, hoping for nothing again; and your reward shall be great, and ye shall be the children of the Highest: for he is kind unto the unthankful and to the evil. Be ye therefore merciful, as your Father also is merciful. Judge not, and ye shall not be judged: condemn not, and ye shall not be condemned: forgive, and ye shall be forgiven.

Luke 6:35-37

Follow peace with all men, and holiness, without which no man shall see the Lord:

Looking diligently lest any man fail of the grace of God; lest any root of bitterness springing up trouble you, and thereby many be defiled.

Hebrews 12:14,15

But if ye have bitter envying and strife in your hearts, glory not, and lie not against the truth.

For where envying and strife is, there is confusion and every evil work. *James 3:14,16*

Let all bitterness, and wrath, and anger, and clamour, and evil speaking, be put away from you, with all malice:

And be ye kind one to another, tenderhearted, forgiving one another, even as God for Christ's sake hath forgiven you. *Ephesians 4:31,32*

And when ye stand praying, forgive, if ye have ought against any: that your Father also which is in heaven may forgive you your trespasses.

Mark 11:25

For thou, Lord, art good, and ready to forgive; and plenteous in mercy unto all them that call upon thee. *Psalm 86:5*

COVENANT BLESSINGS
FOR WHEN I'M:

TEMPTED TO SUICIDE

Thus saith the Lord that made thee, and formed thee from the womb, which will help thee; Fear not....   *Isaiah 44:2*

I know the thoughts that I think toward you, saith the Lord, thoughts of peace, and not of evil, to give you an expected end.   *Jeremiah 29:11*

Be of good courage, and he shall strengthen your heart.   *Psalm 31:24*

Behold, the eye of the Lord is upon them that fear him, upon them that hope in his mercy.
Psalm 33:18

Wherefore he is able also to save them to the uttermost that come unto God by him, seeing he ever liveth to make intercession for them.

Hebrews 7:25

For in thee, O Lord, do I hope: thou wilt hear, O Lord my God.

For I am ready to halt, and my sorrow is continually before me.

For I will declare mine iniquity; I will be sorry for my sin.

Forsake me not, O Lord: O my God, be not far from me.

Make haste to help me, O Lord my salvation.

Psalm 38:15,17,18,21,22

Why art thou cast down, O my soul? and why art thou disquieted in me? hope thou in God: for I shall yet praise him for the help of his countenance.

Psalm 42:5

For we wrestle not against flesh and blood, but against principalities, against powers, against the rulers of the darkness of this world, against spiritual wickedness in high places. *Ephesians 6:12*

For whosoever shall call upon the name of the Lord shall be saved. *Romans 10:13*

Covenant Blessings
For When I'm:

Tense

Trust in the Lord, and do good; so shalt thou dwell in the land, and verily thou shalt be fed.

Delight thyself also in the Lord; and he shall give thee the desires of thine heart.

Commit thy way unto the Lord; trust also in him; and he shall bring it to pass.   *Psalm 37:3-5*

The Lord will give strength unto his people; the Lord will bless his people with peace. *Psalm 29:11*

Be careful for nothing; but in every thing by prayer and supplication with thanksgiving let your requests be made known unto God.

And the peace of God, which passeth all understanding, shall keep your hearts and minds through Christ Jesus.   *Philippians 4:6,7*

Come unto me, all ye that labour and are heavy laden, and I will give you rest.   *Matthew 11:28*

Rest in the Lord, and wait patiently for him: fret not thyself because of him who prospereth in his way, because of the man who bringeth wicked devices to pass.   *Psalm 37:7*

It shall come to pass in the day that the Lord shall give thee rest from thy sorrow, and from thy fear, and from the hard bondage wherein thou wast made to serve.   *Isaiah 14:3*

Let us therefore follow after the things which make for peace.   *Romans 14:19*

Now the God of hope fill you with all joy and peace in believing, that ye may abound in hope, through the power of the Holy Ghost.

Romans 15:13

Covenant Blessings
For When I'm:

Tempted to Worry

Jesus said unto him, If thou canst believe, all things are possible to him that believeth. And straightway the father of the child cried out, and said with tears, Lord, I believe; help thou mine unbelief. *Mark 9:23,24*

Afterward he [Jesus] appeared unto the eleven as they sat at meat, and upbraided them with their unbelief and hardness of heart, because they believed not them which had seen him after he was risen. And he said unto them, Go ye into all the world, and preach the gospel to every creature. He that believeth and is baptized shall be saved; but he that believeth not shall be damned. And these signs shall follow them that believe; In my name shall they cast out devils; they shall speak with new tongues; They shall take up serpents; and if they drink any deadly thing, it shall not hurt them; they shall lay hands on the sick, and they shall recover.

Mark 16:14-18

Therefore I say unto you, What things soever ye desire, when ye pray, believe that ye receive them, and ye shall have them. *Mark 11:24*

Therefore it is of faith, that it might be by grace; to the end the promise might be sure to all the seed; not to that only which is of the law, but to that also which is of the faith of Abraham; who is the father of us all....

He staggered not at the promise of God through unbelief; but was strong in faith, giving glory to God;

And being fully persuaded that, what he had promised, he was able also to perform.

And therefore it was imputed to him for righteousness. *Romans 4:16,20-22*

GOD'S
COVENANT
BLESSINGS
FOR YOU

PART 9

GOD'S
COVENANT
BLESSINGS FOR
WHEN I NEED:

GOD'S COVENANT BLESSINGS
FOR WHEN I NEED:

COMFORT

Blessed are they that mourn: for they shall be comforted.   *Matthew 5:4*

Remember the word unto thy servant, upon which thou hast caused me to hope.

This is my comfort in my affliction: for thy word hath quickened me.   *Psalm 119:49,50*

Let, I pray thee, thy merciful kindness be for my comfort, according to thy word unto thy servant.

Let thy tender mercies come unto me, that I may live.   *Psalm 119:76,77*

The Spirit of the Lord God is upon me; because the Lord hath anointed me...to comfort all that mourn; To appoint unto them that mourn in Zion, to give unto them beauty for ashes, the oil of joy for mourning, the garment of praise for the spirit of heaviness....   *Isaiah 61:1-3*

Blessed be God, even the Father of our Lord Jesus Christ, the Father of mercies, and the God of all comfort;

Who comforteth us in all our tribulation, that we may be able to comfort them which are in any trouble, by the comfort wherewith we ourselves are comforted of God.   *2 Corinthians 1:3,4*

For the Lord himself shall descend from heaven with a shout, with the voice of the archangel, and with the trump of God: and the dead in Christ shall rise first:

Then we which are alive and remain shall be caught up together with them in the clouds to meet the Lord in the air: and so shall we ever be with the Lord.

Wherefore comfort one another with these words.   *1 Thessalonians 4:16-18*

GOD'S COVENANT BLESSINGS
FOR WHEN I NEED:

COURAGE

Be strong and of a good courage, fear not, nor be afraid of them: for the Lord thy God, he it is that doth go with thee; he will not fail thee, nor forsake thee.   *Deuteronomy 31:6*

This book of the law shall not depart out of thy mouth; but thou shalt meditate therein day and night, that thou mayest observe to do according to all that is written therein: for then thou shalt make thy way prosperous, and then thou shalt have good success. Have not I commanded thee? Be strong and of a good courage; be not afraid, neither be thou dismayed: for the Lord thy God is with thee whithersoever thou goest.

Joshua 1:8,9

Be strong and of good courage, and do it: fear not, nor be dismayed: for the Lord God, even my God, will be with thee; he will not fail thee, nor forsake thee, until thou hast finished all the work for the service of the house of the Lord.

1 Chronicles 28:20

O love the Lord, all ye his saints: for the Lord preserveth the faithful, and plentifully rewardeth the proud doer.

Be of good courage, and he shall strengthen your heart, all ye that hope in the Lord.

Psalm 31:23,24

Then shalt thou prosper, if thou takest heed to fulfil the statutes and judgments which the Lord charged Moses with concerning Israel: be strong, and of good courage; dread not, nor be dismayed.

1 Chronicles 22:13

Wait on the Lord: be of good courage, and he shall strengthen thine heart: wait, I say, on the Lord.

Psalm 27:14

GOD'S COVENANT BLESSINGS
FOR WHEN I NEED:

DELIVERANCE

It shall come to pass, that whosoever shall call on the name of the Lord shall be delivered.

Joel 2:32

The seed of the righteous shall be delivered.

Proverbs 11:21

The Spirit of the Lord is upon me, because he hath anointed me...to preach deliverance to the captives, and recovering of sight to the blind, to set at liberty them that are bruised.   *Luke 4:18*

Finally, my brethren, be strong in the Lord, and in the power of his might.

Put on the whole armour of God, that ye may be able to stand against the wiles of the devil.

For we wrestle not against flesh and blood, but against principalities, against powers, against the rulers of the darkness of this world, against spiritual wickedness in high places.

Ephesians 6:10-12

For though we walk in the flesh, we do not war after the flesh.　　　　　*2 Corinthians 10:3*

Behold, I give unto you power to tread on serpents and scorpions, and over all the power of the enemy: and nothing shall by any means hurt you.　　　　　*Luke 10:19*

Ye are of God, little children, and have overcome them: because greater is he that is in you, than he that is in the world.　　　　　*1 John 4:4*

They overcame him by the blood of the Lamb, and by the word of their testimony; and they loved not their lives unto the death.

Revelation 12:11

Submit yourselves therefore to God. Resist the devil, and he will flee from you.   *James 4:7*

GOD'S COVENANT BLESSINGS
FOR WHEN I NEED:

FAITH THAT OVERCOMES

Now faith is the substance of things hoped for, the evidence of things not seen.   *Hebrews 11:1*

For whatsoever is born of God overcometh the world: and this is the victory that overcometh the world, even our faith.   *1 John 5:4*

So then faith cometh by hearing, and hearing by the word of God.   *Romans 10:17*

Therefore I say unto you, What things soever ye desire, when ye pray, believe that ye receive them, and ye shall have them.   *Mark 11:24*

If ye have faith as a grain of mustard seed, ye shall say unto this mountain, Remove hence to yonder place; and it shall remove; and nothing shall be impossible unto you.   *Matthew 17:20*

Jesus saith unto them [the two blind men], Believe ye that I am able to do this? They said unto him, Yea, Lord. Then touched he their eyes, saying, According to your faith be it unto you.

Matthew 9:28,29

Jesus answered and said unto them, Verily I say unto you, If ye have faith, and doubt not, ye shall not only do this which is done to the fig tree, but also if ye shall say unto this mountain, Be thou removed, and be thou cast into the sea; it shall be done. And all things, whatsoever ye shall ask in prayer, believing, ye shall receive.

Matthew 21:21,22

Fight the good fight of faith, lay hold on eternal life, whereunto thou art also called, and hast professed a good profession before many witnesses.

1 Timothy 6:12

God's Covenant Blessings
For When I Need:

Guidance

Teach me thy way, O Lord, and lead me in a plain path, because of mine enemies. *Psalm 27:11*

I will instruct thee and teach thee in the way which thou shalt go: I will guide thee with mine eye.
Psalm 32:8

And thine ears shall hear a word behind thee, saying, This is the way, walk ye in it, when ye turn to the right hand, and when ye turn to the left.
Isaiah 30:21

Trust in the Lord with all thine heart; and lean not unto thine own understanding. In all thy ways acknowledge him, and he shall direct thy paths.
Proverbs 3:5,6

The steps of a good man are ordered by the Lord: and he delighteth in his way. *Psalm 37:23*

For this God is our God for ever and ever: he will be our guide even unto death. *Psalm 48:14*

Through the tender mercy of our God; whereby the dayspring from on high hath visited us, To give light to them that sit in darkness and in the shadow of death, to guide our feet into the way of peace. *Luke 1:78,79*

When he, the Spirit of truth, is come, he will guide you into all truth: for he shall not speak of himself; but whatsoever he shall hear, that shall he speak: and he will shew you things to come.
John 16:13

Nevertheless I am continually with thee: thou hast holden me by my right hand.

Thou shalt guide me with thy counsel, and afterward receive me to glory. *Psalm 73:23,24*

God's Covenant Blessings
For When I Need:

Joy

Thy words were found, and I did eat them; and thy word was unto me the joy and rejoicing of mine heart: for I am called by thy name, O Lord God of hosts.   *Jeremiah 15:16*

But let all those that put their trust in thee rejoice: let them ever shout for joy, because thou defendest them: let them also that love thy name be joyful in thee.   *Psalm 5:11*

Thou wilt shew me the path of life: in thy presence is fulness of joy; at thy right hand there are pleasures for evermore.   *Psalm 16:11*

Weeping may endure for a night, but joy cometh in the morning.   *Psalm 30:5*

They that sow in tears shall reap in joy.

He that goeth forth and weepeth, bearing precious seed, shall doubtless come again with rejoicing, bringing his sheaves with him.

Psalm 126:5,6

The joy of the Lord is your strength.

Nehemiah 8:10

The Spirit of the Lord God is upon me; because the Lord hath anointed me to preach good tidings...To appoint unto them that mourn in Zion, to give unto them beauty for ashes, the oil of joy for mourning, the garment of praise for the spirit of heaviness.   *Isaiah 61:1,3*

If ye keep my commandments, ye shall abide in my love; even as I have kept my Father's commandments, and abide in his love. These things have I spoken unto you, that my joy might remain in you, and that your joy might be full.

John 15:10,11

GOD'S COVENANT BLESSINGS
FOR WHEN I NEED:

GOD'S GRACE IN LONGSUFFERING

The fruit of the Spirit is love, joy, peace, longsuffering, gentleness, goodness, faith,

Meekness, temperance: against such there is no law. *Galatians 5:22,23*

I therefore, the prisoner of the Lord, beseech you that ye walk worthy of the vocation wherewith ye are called,

With all lowliness and meekness, with longsuffering, forbearing one another in love.

Ephesians 4:1,2

For this cause I obtained mercy, that in me first Jesus Christ might shew forth all longsuffering, for a pattern to them which should hereafter believe on him to life everlasting. *1 Timothy 1:16*

Put on therefore, as the elect of God, holy and beloved, bowels of mercies, kindness, humbleness of mind, meekness, longsuffering;

Forbearing one another, and forgiving one another. *Colossians 3:12,13*

For this cause we also, since the day we heard it, do not cease to pray for you, and to desire that ye might be filled with the knowledge of his will in all wisdom and spiritual understanding;

That ye might walk worthy of the Lord unto all pleasing, being fruitful in every good work, and increasing in the knowledge of God;

Strengthened with all might, according to his glorious power, unto all patience and longsuffering with joyfulness. *Colossians 1:9-11*

I charge thee therefore before God, and the Lord Jesus Christ, who shall judge the quick and the dead at his appearing and his kingdom;

Preach the word; be instant in season, out of season; reprove, rebuke, exhort with all longsuffering and doctrine. *2 Timothy 4:1,2*

GOD'S COVENANT BLESSINGS
FOR WHEN I NEED:

LOVE

For God so loved the world, that he gave his only begotten Son, that whosoever believeth in him should not perish, but have everlasting life.

John 3:16

Herein is love, not that we loved God, but that he loved us, and sent his Son to be the propitiation for our sins.

Beloved, if God so loved us, we ought also to love one another.

No man hath seen God at any time. If we love one another, God dwelleth in us, and his love is perfected in us.

There is no fear in love; but perfect love casteth out fear: because fear hath torment. He that feareth is not made perfect in love.

We love him, because he first loved us.

And this commandment have we from him,
That he who loveth God love his brother also.

1 John 4:10-12,18,19,21

Charity suffereth long, and is kind; charity
envieth not; charity vaunteth not itself, is not
puffed up,

Doth not behave itself unseemly, seeketh not
her own, is not easily provoked, thinketh no evil;

Rejoiceth not in iniquity, but rejoiceth in the truth;

Beareth all things, believeth all things, hopeth
all things, endureth all things.

And now abideth faith, hope, charity, these
three; but the greatest of these is charity.

1 Corinthians 13:4-7,13

This is my commandment, That ye love one
another, as I have loved you. Greater love hath no
man than this, that a man lay down his life for his
friends.... These things I command you, that ye
love one another. *John 15:12,13,17*

GOD'S COVENANT BLESSINGS
FOR WHEN I NEED:

PATIENCE

Wait on the Lord: be of good courage, and he shall strengthen thine heart: wait, I say, on the Lord.
Psalm 27:14

They that wait upon the Lord shall renew their strength; they shall mount up with wings as eagles; they shall run, and not be weary; and they shall walk, and not faint. *Isaiah 40:31*

For whatsoever things were written aforetime were written for our learning, that we through patience and comfort of the scriptures might have hope. *Romans 15:4*

And the Lord direct your hearts into the love of God, and into the patient waiting for Christ.
2 Thessalonians 3:5

And we desire that every one of you do shew the same diligence to the full assurance of hope unto the end:

That ye be not slothful, but followers of them who through faith and patience inherit the promises.

Hebrews 6:11,12

Cast not away therefore your confidence, which hath great recompence of reward.

For ye have need of patience, that, after ye have done the will of God, ye might receive the promise.

Hebrews 10:35,36

Wherefore seeing we also are compassed about with so great a cloud of witnesses, let us lay aside every weight, and the sin which doth so easily beset us, and let us run with patience the race that is set before us.

Hebrews 12:1

My brethren, count it all joy when ye fall into divers temptations;

Knowing this, that the trying of your faith worketh patience.

But let patience have her perfect work, that ye may be perfect and entire, wanting nothing.

James 1:2-4

GOD'S COVENANT BLESSINGS
FOR WHEN I NEED:

PEACE

The Lord will give strength unto his people; the Lord will bless his people with peace.

Psalm 29:11

Great peace have they which love thy law: and nothing shall offend them.   *Psalm 119:165*

Let us therefore follow after the things which make for peace.   *Romans 14:19*

Thou wilt keep him in perfect peace, whose mind is stayed on thee: because he trusteth in thee.

Isaiah 26:3

I will both lay me down in peace, and sleep: for thou, Lord, only makest me dwell in safety.

Psalm 4:8

And the work of righteousness shall be peace; and the effect of righteousness quietness and assurance for ever.   *Isaiah 32:17*

When a man's ways please the Lord, he maketh even his enemies to be at peace with him.
Proverbs 16:7

He hath delivered my soul in peace from the battle that was against me.   *Psalm 55:18*

Peace I leave with you, my peace I give unto you: not as the world giveth, give I unto you. Let not your heart be troubled, neither let it be afraid.
John 14:27

Therefore being justified by faith, we have peace with God through our Lord Jesus Christ.
Romans 5:1

Be careful for nothing; but in every thing by prayer and supplication with thanksgiving let your requests be made known unto God.

And the peace of God, which passeth all understanding, shall keep your hearts and minds through Christ Jesus. *Philippians 4:6,7*

God's Covenant Blessings
For When I Need:

Strength

Fear thou not; for I am with thee: be not dismayed; for I am thy God: I will strengthen thee; yea, I will help thee; yea, I will uphold thee with the right hand of my righteousness.

Isaiah 41:10

Have not I commanded thee? Be strong and of a good courage; be not afraid, neither be thou dismayed: for the Lord thy God is with thee whithersoever thou goest.   *Joshua 1:9*

For the joy of the Lord is your strength.

Nehemiah 8:10

And as thy days, so shall thy strength be.

Deuteronomy 33:25

Seek the Lord and his strength, seek his face continually.... Glory and honour are in his presence; strength and gladness are in his place.

1 Chronicles 16:11,27

Both riches and honour come of thee, and thou reignest over all; and in thine hand is power and might; and in thine hand it is to make great, and to give strength unto all.   *1 Chronicles 29:12*

The Lord will give strength unto his people; the Lord will bless his people with peace. *Psalm 29:11*

I can do all things through Christ which strength-eneth me.   *Philippians 4:13*

Let the weak say, I am strong.   *Joel 3:10*

Wait on the Lord: be of good courage, and he shall strengthen thine heart: wait, I say, on the Lord.

Psalm 27:14

God is our refuge and strength, a very present help in trouble.   *Psalm 46:1*

GOD'S COVENANT BLESSINGS
FOR WHEN I NEED:

TEMPERANCE

And every man that striveth for the mastery is temperate in all things. Now they do it to obtain a corruptible crown; but we an incorruptible.

But I keep under my body, and bring it into subjection: lest that by any means, when I have preached to others, I myself should be a castaway.

1 Corinthians 9:25,27

For the kingdom of God is not meat and drink; but righteousness, and peace, and joy in the Holy Ghost. *Romans 14:17*

And beside this, giving all diligence, add to your faith virtue; and to virtue knowledge;

And to knowledge temperance; and to temperance patience; and to patience godliness.

2 Peter 1:5,6

Let your moderation be known unto all men. The Lord is at hand.   *Philippians 4:5*

Therefore let us not sleep, as do others; but let us watch and be sober.

For they that sleep sleep in the night; and they that be drunken are drunken in the night.

But let us, who are of the day, be sober, putting on the breastplate of faith and love; and for an helmet, the hope of salvation.

                                    1 Thessalonians 5:6-8

For the grace of God that bringeth salvation hath appeared to all men,

Teaching us that, denying ungodliness and worldly lusts, we should live soberly, righteously, and godly, in this present world.   *Titus 2:11,12*

God's Covenant Blessings
For When I Need:

To Be Forgiven

For thou, Lord, art good, and ready to forgive; and plenteous in mercy unto all them that call upon thee. *Psalm 86:5*

Thou hast forgiven the iniquity of thy people, thou hast covered all their sin. Selah.

Psalm 85:2

Blessed is he whose transgression is forgiven, whose sin is covered. *Psalm 32:1*

Therefore if any man be in Christ, he is a new creature: old things are passed away; behold, all things are become new. *2 Corinthians 5:17*

In whom we have redemption through his

blood, the forgiveness of sins, according to the riches of his grace. *Ephesians 1:7*

As far as the east is from the west, so far hath he removed our transgressions from us. *Psalm 103:12*

My little children, these things write I unto you, that ye sin not. And if any man sin, we have an advocate with the Father, Jesus Christ the righteous.
1 John 2:1

If we confess our sins, he is faithful and just to forgive us our sins, and to cleanse us from all unrighteousness. *1 John 1:9*

I, even I, am he that blotteth out thy transgressions for mine own sake, and will not remember thy sins. *Isaiah 43:25*

Come now, and let us reason together, saith the Lord: though your sins be as scarlet, they shall be as white as snow; though they be red like crimson, they shall be as wool. *Isaiah 1:18*

GOD'S COVENANT BLESSINGS
FOR WHEN I NEED:

TO FORGIVE

Put on therefore, as the elect of God, holy and beloved, bowels of mercies, kindness, humbleness of mind, meekness, longsuffering;

Forbearing one another, and forgiving one another, if any man have a quarrel against any: even as Christ forgave you, so also do ye.

Colossians 3:12,13

Judge not, and ye shall not be judged: condemn not, and ye shall not be condemned: forgive, and ye shall be forgiven.   *Luke 6:37*

Therefore if thou bring thy gift to the altar, and there rememberest that thy brother hath ought against thee; Leave there thy gift before the altar, and go thy way; first be reconciled to thy brother, and then come and offer thy gift.

Matthew 5:23,24

If ye forgive men their trespasses, your heavenly Father will also forgive you: But if ye forgive not men their trespasses, neither will your Father forgive your trespasses. *Matthew 6:14,15*

Then came Peter to him, and said, Lord, how oft shall my brother sin against me, and I forgive him? till seven times? Jesus saith unto him, I say not unto thee, Until seven times: but, Until seventy times seven. *Matthew 18:21,22*

Let all bitterness, and wrath, and anger, and clamour, and evil speaking, be put away from you, with all malice:

And be ye kind one to another, tenderhearted, forgiving one another, even as God for Christ's sake hath forgiven you.

Ephesians 4:31,32

GOD'S COVENANT BLESSINGS
FOR WHEN I NEED:

WISDOM

If any of you lack wisdom, let him ask of God, that giveth to all men liberally, and upbraideth not; and it shall be given him.   *James 1:5*

For the Lord giveth wisdom: out of his mouth cometh knowledge and understanding. He layeth up sound wisdom for the righteous. *Proverbs 2:6,7*

Give instruction to a wise man, and he will be yet wiser: teach a just man, and he will increase in learning. The fear of the Lord is the beginning of wisdom: and the knowledge of the holy is understanding.   *Proverbs 9:9,10*

A wise man will hear, and will increase learning; and a man of understanding shall attain unto wise counsels.   *Proverbs 1:5*

The way of a fool is right in his own eyes: but he that hearkeneth unto counsel is wise.

Proverbs 12:15

Hear counsel, and receive instruction, that thou mayest be wise in thy latter end.

Proverbs 19:20

For by wise counsel thou shalt make thy war: and in multitude of counsellors there is safety.

Proverbs 24:6

These things also belong to the wise. It is not good to have respect of persons in judgment.

Proverbs 24:23

A fool uttereth all his mind: but a wise man keepeth it in till afterwards.   *Proverbs 29:11*

See then that ye walk circumspectly, not as fools, but as wise,

Redeeming the time, because the days are evil.

Wherefore be ye not unwise, but understanding what the will of the Lord is.   *Ephesians 5:15-17*

GOD'S
COVENANT
BLESSINGS
FOR YOU

PART 10

GOD'S
COVENANT WORD
REVEALS WHAT
HE WANTS ME
TO DO TODAY

GOD WANTS ME
TO UNDERSTAND
HIS COVENANT BY:

SPENDING TIME IN HIS WORD

All scripture is given by inspiration of God, and is profitable for doctrine, for reproof, for correction, for instruction in righteousness:

That the man of God may be perfect, throughly furnished unto all good works. *2 Timothy 3:16,17*

This book of the law shall not depart out of thy mouth; but thou shalt meditate therein day and night, that thou mayest observe to do according to all that is written therein: for then thou shalt make thy way prosperous, and then thou shalt have good success. *Joshua 1:8*

Blessed is the man that walketh not in the counsel of the ungodly, nor standeth in the way of sinners, nor sitteth in the seat of the scornful.

But his delight is in the law of the Lord; and in his law doth he meditate day and night.

And he shall be like a tree planted by the rivers of water, that bringeth forth his fruit in his season; his leaf also shall not wither; and whatsoever he doeth shall prosper.   *Psalm 1:1-3*

Whereby are given unto us exceeding great and precious promises: that by these ye might be partakers of the divine nature.   *2 Peter 1:4*

When thou goest, it shall lead thee; when thou sleepest, it shall keep thee; and when thou awakest, it shall talk with thee. For the commandment is a lamp; and the law is light; and reproofs of instruction are the way of life.

Proverbs 6:22,23

Let them not depart from thine eyes; keep them in the midst of thine heart. For they are life unto those that find them, and health to all their flesh.

Proverbs 4:21,22

GOD WANTS ME
TO UNDERSTAND
HIS COVENANT BY:

TALKING TO HIM IN PRAYER

I exhort therefore, that, first of all, supplications, prayers, intercessions, and giving of thanks, be made for all men;....

For this is good and acceptable in the sight of God our Saviour;....

I will therefore that men pray every where, lifting up holy hands, without wrath and doubting.

1 Timothy 2:1,3,8

Verily, verily, I say unto you, Whatsoever ye shall ask the Father in my name, he will give it you. Hitherto have ye asked nothing in my name: ask, and ye shall receive, that your joy may be full.

John 16:23,24

If ye abide in me, and my words abide in you, ye shall ask what ye will, and it shall be done unto you. *John 15:7*

And whatsoever we ask, we receive of him, because we keep his commandments, and do those things that are pleasing in his sight.
1 John 3:22

And this is the confidence that we have in him, that, if we ask any thing according to his will, he heareth us:

And if we know that he hear us, whatsoever we ask, we know that we have the petitions that we desired of him. *1 John 5:14,15*

Ask, and it shall be given you; seek, and ye shall find; knock, and it shall be opened unto you: For every one that asketh receiveth; and he that seeketh findeth; and to him that knocketh it shall be opened. *Matthew 7:7,8*

Let us therefore come boldly unto the throne of grace, that we may obtain mercy, and find grace to help in time of need.   *Hebrews 4:16*

God Wants Me
To Understand
His Covenant by:

Walking in Fellowship

Truly our fellowship is with the Father, and with his Son Jesus Christ.

If we say that we have fellowship with him, and walk in darkness, we lie, and do not the truth:

But if we walk in the light, as he is in the light, we have fellowship one with another, and the blood of Jesus Christ his Son cleanseth us from all sin.   *1 John 1:3,6,7*

God is faithful, by whom ye were called unto the fellowship of his Son Jesus Christ our Lord.

Now I beseech you, brethren, by the name of our Lord Jesus Christ, that ye all speak the same thing, and that there be no divisions among you; but that ye be perfectly joined together in the same mind and in the same judgment.   *1 Corinthians 1:9,10*

Bear ye one another's burdens, and so fulfill the law of Christ.

As we have therefore opportunity, let us do good unto all men, especially unto them who are of the household of faith.   *Galatians 6:2,10*

Let your conversation be as it becometh the gospel of Christ: that whether I come and see you, or else be absent, I may hear of your affairs, that ye stand fast in one spirit, with one mind striving together for the faith of the gospel.

Philippians 1:27

I say unto you, That if two of you shall agree on earth as touching any thing that they shall ask, it shall be done for them of my Father which is in heaven. For where two or three are gathered together in my name, there am I in the midst of them.   *Matthew 18:19,20*

God Wants Me
To Understand
His Covenant by:

Being Conformed
to His Image

I am crucified with Christ: nevertheless I live;
yet not I, but Christ liveth in me: and the life
which I now live in the flesh I live by the faith of
the Son of God, who loved me, and gave himself
for me.   *Galatians 2:20*

Lie not one to another, seeing that ye have put
off the old man with his deeds;

And have put on the new man, which is
renewed in knowledge after the image of him
that created him.   *Colossians 3:9,10*

What? know ye not that your body is the
temple of the Holy Ghost which is in you, which
ye have of God, and ye are not your own?

For ye are bought with a price: therefore glorify God in your body, and in your spirit, which are God's.   *1 Corinthians 6:19,20*

I beseech you therefore, brethren, by the mercies of God, that ye present your bodies a living sacrifice, holy, acceptable unto God, which is your reasonable service.

And be not conformed to this world: but be ye transformed by the renewing of your mind, that ye may prove what is that good, and acceptable, and perfect, will of God.   *Romans 12:1,2*

For whom he did foreknow, he also did predestinate to be conformed to the image of his Son.
Romans 8:29

And as we have borne the image of the earthy, we shall also bear the image of the heavenly.
1 Corinthians 15:49

But we all, with open face beholding as in a glass the glory of the Lord, are changed into the same image from glory to glory, even as by the Spirit of the Lord.   *2 Corinthians 3:18*

GOD WANTS ME
TO UNDERSTAND
HIS COVENANT BY:

GIVING HIM PRAISE
AND WORSHIP

Oh that men would praise the Lord for his goodness, and for his wonderful works to the children of men! *Psalm 107:8*

For the Lord is great, and greatly to be praised. *Psalm 96:4*

O clap your hands, all ye people; shout unto God with the voice of triumph. *Psalm 47:1*

Rejoice in the Lord alway: and again I say, Rejoice. *Philippians 4:4*

Praise him with the sound of the trumpet: praise him with the psaltery and harp.

Praise him with the timbrel and dance: praise him with stringed instruments and organs.

Praise him upon the loud cymbals: praise him upon the high sounding cymbals.

Let every thing that hath breath praise the Lord. Praise ye the Lord.   *Psalm 150:3-6*

Let the people praise thee, O God; let all the people praise thee.   *Psalm 67:5*

O come, let us worship and bow down: let us kneel before the Lord our maker.   *Psalm 95:6*

I will praise the name of God with a song, and will magnify him with thanksgiving. *Psalm 69:30*

While I live will I praise the Lord: I will sing praises unto my God while I have any being.

Psalm 146:2

From the rising of the sun unto the going down of the same the Lord's name is to be praised.

Psalm 113:3

By him therefore let us offer the sacrifice of praise to God continually.   *Hebrews 13:15*

GOD WANTS ME
TO UNDERSTAND
HIS COVENANT BY:

BEING FILLED
WITH HIS GLORY

And it came to pass, when Moses came down from mount Sinai with the two tables of testimony in Moses' hand, when he came down from the mount, that Moses wist not that the skin of his face shone while he talked with him. And when Aaron and all the children of Israel saw Moses, behold, the skin of his face shone; and they were afraid to come nigh him.... And till Moses had done speaking with them, he put a vail on his face.   *Exodus 34:29,30,33*

Arise, shine; for thy light is come, and the glory of the Lord is risen upon thee. For, behold, the darkness shall cover the earth, and gross darkness the people: but the Lord shall arise upon thee, and his glory shall be seen upon thee. And the Gentiles shall come to thy light, and kings to the brightness of thy rising. *Isaiah 60:1-3*

Then shall thy light break forth as the morning, and thine health shall spring forth speedily: and thy righteousness shall go before thee; the glory of the Lord shall be thy rearward.
Isaiah 58:8

For the earth shall be filled with the knowledge of the glory of the Lord, as the waters cover the sea. *Habakkuk 2:14*

Unto him be glory in the church by Christ Jesus throughout all ages, world without end. Amen.
Ephesians 3:21

If thy whole body therefore be full of light, having no part dark, the whole shall be full of light, as when the bright shining of a candle doth give thee light. *Luke 11:36*

But we all, with open face beholding as in a glass the glory of the Lord, are changed into the same image from glory to glory, even as by the Spirit of the Lord.   *2 Corinthians 3:18*

God Wants Me
To Understand
His Covenant by:

Expecting His Return

In my Father's house are many mansions: if it were not so, I would have told you. I go to prepare a place for you. And if I go and prepare a place for you, I will come again, and receive you unto myself; that where I am, there ye may be also.

John 14:2,3

Ye men of Galilee, why stand ye gazing up into heaven? this same Jesus, which is taken up from you into heaven, shall so come in like manner as ye have seen him go into heaven.

Acts 1:11

Be patient therefore, brethren, unto the coming of the Lord. Behold, the husbandman waiteth for the precious fruit of the earth, and hath long patience for it, until he receive the early and latter rain.

Be ye also patient; stablish your hearts: for the coming of the Lord draweth nigh.   *James 5:7,8*

...We should live soberly, righteously, and godly, in this present world;

Looking for that blessed hope, and the glorious appearing of the great God and our Saviour Jesus Christ.   *Titus 2:12,13*

Beloved, be not ignorant of this one thing, that one day is with the Lord as a thousand years, and a thousand years as one day.

But the day of the Lord will come as a thief in the night; in the which the heavens shall pass away with a great noise, and the elements shall melt with fervent heat, the earth also and the works that are therein shall be burned up.

2 Peter 3:8,10

When the Son of man shall come in his glory, and all the holy angels with him, then shall he sit upon the throne of his glory. *Matthew 25:31*

GOD WANTS ME
TO FULFILL HIS
COVENANT BY:

LIVING BY FAITH

Now faith is the substance of things hoped for, the evidence of things not seen.

Through faith we understand that the worlds were framed by the word of God, so that things which are seen were not made of things which do appear. *Hebrews 11:1,3*

So then faith cometh by hearing, and hearing by the word of God. *Romans 10:17*

Jesus said unto him, If thou canst believe, all things are possible to him that believeth. *Mark 9:23*

For whatsoever is born of God overcometh the world: and this is the victory that overcometh the world, even our faith. *1 John 5:4*

And Jesus answering saith unto them, Have faith in God. For verily I say unto you, That whosoever shall say unto this mountain, Be thou removed, and be thou cast into the sea; and shall not doubt in his heart, but shall believe that those things which he saith shall come to pass; he shall have whatsoever he saith. *Mark 11:22,23*

Who through faith subdued kingdoms, wrought righteousness, obtained promises, stopped the mouths of lions,

Quenched the violence of fire, escaped the edge of the sword, out of weakness were made strong, waxed valiant in fight, turned to flight the armies of the aliens. *Hebrews 11:33,34*

But without faith it is impossible to please him: for he that cometh to God must believe that he is, and that he is a rewarder of them that diligently seek him. *Hebrews 11:6*

GOD WANTS ME
TO FULFILL HIS
COVENANT BY:

LIVING IN OBEDIENCE

And it shall come to pass, if thou shalt hearken diligently unto the voice of the Lord thy God, to observe and to do all his commandments which I command thee this day, that the Lord thy God will set thee on high above all nations of the earth: And all these blessings shall come on thee, and overtake thee.   *Deuteronomy 28:1,2*

Behold, to obey is better than sacrifice, and to hearken than the fat of rams. For rebellion is as the sin of witchcraft, and stubbornness is as iniquity and idolatry.   *1 Samuel 15:22,23*

Now therefore, if ye will obey my voice indeed, and keep my covenant, then ye shall be a peculiar treasure unto me above all people: for all the earth is mine.   *Exodus 19:5*

Know ye not, that to whom ye yield yourselves servants to obey, his servants ye are to whom ye obey; whether of sin unto death, or of obedience unto righteousness? *Romans 6:16*

For the time is come that judgment must begin at the house of God: and if it first begin at us, what shall the end be of them that obey not the gospel of God? *1 Peter 4:17*

Submit yourselves therefore to God. Resist the devil, and he will flee from you. *James 4:7*

Obey my voice, and I will be your God, and ye shall be my people: and walk ye in all the ways that I have commanded you, that it may be well unto you. *Jeremiah 7:23*

And whatsoever we ask, we receive of him, because we keep his commandments, and do those things that are pleasing in his sight. *1 John 3:22*

GOD WANTS ME
TO FULFILL HIS
COVENANT BY:

LIVING IN THE
POWER OF HIS SPIRIT

Jesus answered, Verily, verily, I say unto thee, Except a man be born of water and of the Spirit, he cannot enter into the kingdom of God.   *John 3:5*

Not that we are sufficient of our selves to think any thing as of ourselves; but our sufficiency is of God;

Who also hath made us able ministers of the new testament; not of the letter, but of the spirit: for the letter killeth, but the spirit giveth life.

2 Corinthians 3:5,6

It is the spirit that quickeneth.   *John 6:63*

Walk in the Spirit, and ye shall not fulfil the lust of the flesh.

For the flesh lusteth against the Spirit, and the Spirit against the flesh: and these are contrary the one to the other: so that ye cannot do the things that ye would. *Galatians 5:16,17*

There is therefore now no condemnation to them which are in Christ Jesus, who walk not after the flesh, but after the Spirit.

For as many as are led by the Spirit of God, they are the sons of God. *Romans 8:1,14*

God anointed Jesus of Nazareth with the Holy Ghost and with power. *Acts 10:38*

Ye shall receive power, after that the Holy Ghost is come upon you. *Acts 1:8*

But the fruit of the Spirit is love, joy, peace, longsuffering, gentleness, goodness, faith,

Meekness, temperance: against such there is no law.

If we live in the Spirit, let us also walk in the Spirit. *Galatians 5:22,23,25*

GOD WANTS ME
TO FULFILL HIS
COVENANT BY:

WALKING IN LOVE

Walk in love, as Christ also hath loved us, and hath given himself for us an offering and a sacrifice to God for a sweetsmelling savour.

Ephesians 5:2

God is love; and he that dwelleth in love dwelleth in God, and God in him.   *1 John 4:16*

And thou shalt love the Lord thy God with all thy heart, and with all thy soul, and with all thy mind, and with all thy strength: this is the first commandment. And the second is like, namely this, Thou shalt love thy neighbour as thyself. There is none other commandment greater than these.

Mark 12:30,31

For if ye love them which love you, what thank have ye? for sinners also love those that love them.... But love ye your enemies, and do good, and lend, hoping for nothing again; and your reward shall be great, and ye shall be the children of the Highest: for he is kind unto the unthankful and to the evil. *Luke 6:32,35*

This is my commandment, That ye love one another, as I have loved you. Greater love hath no man than this, that a man lay down his life for his friends.... These things I command you, that ye love one another. *John 15:12,13,17*

The love of God is shed abroad in our hearts by the Holy Ghost which is given unto us. *Romans 5:5*

And we know that all things work together for good to them that love God, to them who are the called according to his purpose. *Romans 8:28*

But as it is written, Eye hath not seen, nor ear heard, neither have entered into the heart of man, the things which God hath prepared for them that love him.   *1 Corinthians 2:9*

GOD WANTS ME
TO FULFILL HIS
COVENANT BY:

REACHING OUT TO OTHERS

Then shall the King say unto them on his right hand, Come, ye blessed of my Father, inherit the kingdom prepared for you from the foundation of the world: For I was an hungred, and ye gave me meat: I was thirsty, and ye gave me drink: I was a stranger, and ye took me in: Naked, and ye clothed me: I was sick, and ye visited me: I was in prison, and ye came unto me.... And the King shall answer and say unto them, Verily I say unto you, Inasmuch as ye have done it unto one of the least of these my brethren, ye have done it unto me.

Matthew 25:34-36,40

For whosoever shall give you a cup of water to drink in my name, because ye belong to

Christ, verily I say unto you, he shall not lose his reward. *Mark 9:41*

Be not forgetful to entertain strangers: for thereby some have entertained angels unawares. *Hebrews 13:2*

Withhold not good from them to whom it is due, when it is in the power of thine hand to do it. Say not unto thy neighbour, Go, and come again, and to morrow I will give; when thou hast it by thee. *Proverbs 3:27,28*

Love your enemies, bless them that curse you, do good to them that hate you, and pray for them which despitefully use you, and persecute you. *Matthew 5:44*

Knowing that whatsoever good thing any man doeth, the same shall he receive of the Lord, whether he be bond or free. *Ephesians 6:8*

GOD WANTS ME
TO FULFILL HIS
COVENANT BY:

BEING A WITNESS FOR HIM

Go ye therefore, and teach all nations, baptizing them in the name of the Father, and of the Son, and of the Holy Ghost: Teaching them to observe all things whatsoever I have commanded you: and, lo, I am with you alway, even unto the end of the world.   *Matthew 28:19,20*

But ye shall receive power, after that the Holy Ghost is come upon you: and ye shall be witnesses unto me both in Jerusalem, and in all Judaea, and in Samaria, and unto the uttermost part of the earth.   *Acts 1:8*

By the hands of the apostles were many signs and wonders wrought among the people;.... And believers were the more added to the Lord, multitudes both of men and women.

Acts 5:12,14

The things that thou hast heard of me among many witnesses, the same commit thou to faithful men, who shall be able to teach others also.

2 Timothy 2:2

For so hath the Lord commanded us, saying, I have set thee to be a light of the Gentiles, that thou shouldest be for salvation unto the ends of the earth. *Acts 13:47*

For thou shalt be his witness unto all men of what thou hast seen and heard. *Acts 22:15*

This gospel of the kingdom shall be preached in all the world for a witness unto all nations; and then shall the end come. *Matthew 24:14*

But ye are a chosen generation, a royal priesthood, an holy nation, a peculiar people; that ye should shew forth the praises of him who hath called you out of darkness into marvellous light.

1 Peter 2:9

GOD WANTS ME
TO FULFILL HIS
COVENANT BY:

LIVING IN VICTORY

Finally, my brethren, be strong in the Lord, and in the power of his might.

Put on the whole armour of God, that ye may be able to stand against the wiles of the devil.

For we wrestle not against flesh and blood, but against principalities, against powers, against the rulers of the darkness of this world, against spiritual wickedness in high places.

Wherefore take unto you the whole armour of God, that ye may be able to withstand in the evil day, and having done all, to stand.

Stand therefore, having your loins girt about with truth, and having on the breastplate of righteousness;

And your feet shod with the preparation of the gospel of peace;

Above all, taking the shield of faith, wherewith

ye shall be able to quench all the fiery darts of the wicked.

And take the helmet of salvation, and the sword of the Spirit, which is the word of God.

Ephesians 6:10-17

Who shall separate us from the love of Christ? shall tribulation, or distress, or persecution, or famine, or nakedness, or peril, or sword?

Nay, in all these things we are more than conquerors through him that loved us.

Romans 8:35,37

No weapon that is formed against thee shall prosper; and every tongue that shall rise against thee in judgment thou shalt condemn. This is the heritage of the servants of the Lord, and their righteousness is of me, saith the Lord.

Isaiah 54:17

For whatsoever is born of God overcometh the world: and this is the victory that overcometh the world, even our faith.   *1 John 5:4*

GOD'S
COVENANT
BLESSINGS
FOR YOU

PART 11

GOD'S
COVENANT
BLESSINGS FOR
ETERNAL LIFE

GOD'S COVENANT BLESSINGS
FOR ETERNAL LIFE:

COVENANT PROMISES
FOR SALVATION

He that believeth and is baptized shall be saved; but he that believeth not shall be damned.

Mark 16:16

It shall come to pass, that whosoever shall call on the name of the Lord shall be saved.

Acts 2:21

Neither is there salvation in any other: for there is none other name under heaven given among men, whereby we must be saved.

Acts 4:12

And [the keeper of the prison] brought them out, and said, Sirs, what must I do to be saved? And they [Paul and Silas] said, Believe on the

Lord Jesus Christ, and thou shalt be saved, and thy house. *Acts 16:30,31*

That if thou shalt confess with thy mouth the Lord Jesus, and shalt believe in thine heart that God hath raised him from the dead, thou shalt be saved.

For whosoever shall call upon the name of the Lord shall be saved. *Romans 10:9,13*

For the preaching of the cross is to them that perish foolishness; but unto us which are saved it is the power of God. *1 Corinthians 1:18*

For by grace are ye saved through faith; and that not of yourselves: it is the gift of God:

Not of works, lest any man should boast.

Ephesians 2:8,9

Christ hath redeemed us from the curse of the law, being made a curse for us: for it is written, Cursed is every one that hangeth on a tree.

Galatians 3:13

For God sent not his Son into the world to condemn the world; but that the world through him might be saved.   *John 3:17*

INDEX

ABOUT THE AUTHOR

A.L. Gill is the author of the best-selling book, *God's Promises for Your Every Need*, with millions of copies in print. He and his wife, Joyce, have co-authored eighteen books and manuals which are now in several languages.

He believes it is the power of God's Word that changes lives and brings victory. It is God's Word that will go forth and not return void. It is God's Word that will accomplish what it was sent to do!

Dr. Gill has preached to crowds as large as three hundred thousand. His ministry is based strongly on the Word of God. His vision is to equip believers everywhere to do the same works Jesus did.

His ministry travels have taken him to over sixty nations where millions have been touched by the power of God through crusades, seminars and Bible school ministry. His teaching on audio and video tapes has been translated into over thirty-five languages and is going around the world reaching places where it is impossible to minister in person.

To contact A. L. Gill,
write:

A. L. Gill
Gill Ministries
P. O. Box 99
Fawnskin, California 92333

*Please include your prayer requests
and comments when you write.*

Additional copies of this book
available from your local bookstore.

HARRISON HOUSE
Tulsa, Oklahoma 74153

The Harrison House Vision

Proclaiming the truth and the power
Of the Gospel of Jesus Christ
With excellence;
Challenging Christians to
Live victoriously,
Grow spiritually,
Know God intimately.